YOU
WILL
LIVE
FOREVER

YOU WILL LIVE FOREVER

D.L. Moody

Whitaker House

All Scripture quotations are from the *King James Version* (KJV) of the Bible.

YOU WILL LIVE FOREVER

ISBN: 0-88368-307-5
Printed in the United States of America
Copyright © 1997 by Whitaker House

Whitaker House
30 Hunt Valley Circle
New Kensington, PA 15063

1 2 3 4 5 6 7 8 9 10 11   2 / 07 06 05 04 03 02 01 00 99 98 97

Contents

Chapter 1

Christ's Boundless Compassion

The Bible reveals that Jesus often was moved with compassion. We are told in the fourteenth chapter of Matthew that the disciples of John the Baptist came to Him and told Him that their master had been put to a cruel death, that he had been beheaded. When Jesus heard this, He went out to a remote area. A large number of people followed Him, and when He saw them He was *"moved with compassion toward them, and he healed their sick"* (v. 14).

When the people gathered around Jesus, He knew all about their weary, broken, and aching hearts. And if Jesus were with you in person right now, looking intently into your face, His heart would be moved because He would also look into your heart and see the burdens and troubles and sorrows you have to bear. They are hidden from me, but He knows about them. And He is with you now, although you cannot see Him with your physical eye. There is not a sorrow or trouble or affliction that you are enduring that He does not know all about. He is the same today as He was when He was here on earth—the same Jesus, the same Man of compassion.

When He saw that multitude, He had compassion on them and healed their sick. I hope He will heal a great many sin-sick souls and will bind up a great many broken hearts in those who are reading this book. There is no one whose heart is bruised and broken that the Son of God will not have compassion on—if you will let Him. *"A bruised reed shall he not break, and the smoking flax shall he not quench"* (Isa. 42:3). He came into the world to bring mercy, joy, compassion, and love.

If I were an artist, I would draw some pictures and present you with an idea of what that great crowd of people were like, those on whom our Lord had compassion. I would draw another picture of the man who is mentioned in the first chapter of Mark, who came to Jesus full of leprosy from head to foot. There he was, banished from his home and from his friends, and he came to Jesus with his sad and miserable story.

This is the kind of person on whom Jesus has compassion. So that we can understand the full implications of this, we need to make the biblical accounts come alive to us. They need to be recognized as real events, for that is what they were.

THE LEPER HEALED

Just think about that leper. Think about how much he had suffered. I don't know how many years he had been away from his wife and children and home, but there he was, an outcast, a leper. He had to wear strange and distinctive clothing, so that anybody who came near him would know that he was unclean. If he saw anyone approaching him, he had to cry out in warning, "Unclean! Unclean! Unclean!" Yes, and if the wife of his heart were to come out to tell him that their beloved child was sick and dying, he would not dare come near her; he was obligated to run away. He might be able to hear her voice from a distance, but he could not be there to see his child in its last dying moments.

He was, as it were, in a living sepulcher. It was worse than death. There he was, dying by inches, an outcast from everybody and everything, and no one would put out a hand to relieve him. What a terrible life!

Then, imagine him coming to Christ. When Christ sees him, He is *"moved with compassion"* (Mark 1:41). He has a heart that beats in sympathy with the poor leper. The man comes to Him and says, *"If thou wilt, thou canst make me clean"* (v. 40). He knows that no one can make him clean except the Son of God Himself. And the great heart of Christ is moved with compassion toward him. Hear His gracious words: *"I will; be thou clean"* (v. 41). Immediately, the leprosy flees, and the man is made whole.

Look at the man now—no longer an outcast, no longer a loathsome thing, no longer cursed with that terrible leprous disease— rejoicing as he goes back home to his wife and children and friends!

Now, my friend, you may say you pity a man who was that bad off, but did it ever strike you that you are a thousand times worse off than he was? The leprosy of the soul is far worse than the leprosy of the body. I would a thousand times rather have my body full of leprosy than go down to hell with my soul full of sin. It would be much better for me to have my right hand lopped off, to have my right foot decay, and to be lame and blind all the days of my life, than to be banished from God by the leprosy of sin.

Hear the wailing and the agony and the anguish, caused by sin, that is going up from this earth! If there is one poor soul reading this book who is filled with the leprosy of sin, I urge you to come to Christ, and He will have compassion on you. He will say to you, as He did to that man, *"Be thou clean."*

THE DEAD RAISED

Let us look at another picture, from the seventh chapter of Luke, that shows how Jesus was moved with compassion.

Imagine that you can see into a little home in Nain, a village of Galilee. There is a poor widow sitting there. Perhaps it was only a few months earlier that she had buried her husband, but she has an only son left. How she dotes on him! She looks to him to be her strength and support and friend in her old age. She loves him far better than her own life. But then sickness enters the dwelling and Death comes with it and lays his ice-cold hand on the young man. You can see that widowed mother watching over him day and night. Finally, his eyes are closed and his beloved voice is silenced, she thinks, forever. She will never see or hear him anymore after he is buried out of her sight.

And so, it comes time for his burial. Many of you have mourned with your friends and have been with them when they have gone to the cemetery and looked at their loved one for the last time. I imagine there is not one person reading this book who has not lost some loved one. I have never gone to a funeral and seen a mother take her last look at her child without it piercing my heart, and I cannot keep back the tears at such a sight.

Well, the mother kisses her only son on that poor, icy forehead. It is her last kiss, her last look. The body is covered up and they put it on the bier and start for the place of burial, accompanied by a large crowd. The woman has a great many friends. The little town of Nain is moved at the sight of the widow's only son being carried to his place of burial.

Picture that great crowd of people as they come pushing out of the gates of the town. A little farther up the road are thirteen men who are weary and dusty and tired, and they have to stand by the side of the road to let this great crowd pass by. The Son of God is in this group, and the others with Him are His disciples.

Jesus looks on that scene and sees the mother with her broken heart. He sees it bleeding, crushed, and wounded, and it touches His heart. Yes, the great heart of the Son of

God is moved with compassion He comes up and touches the bier and says. "Young man, arise!" and the young man sits up.

I can see the startled and astonished crowd. I can see the widowed mother going back home rejoicing, with the morning rays of the resurrection shining in her heart. Yes, He had compassion on her, indeed! And, if you are a widow, Christ will respond to your troubles and give you peace. Oh, dear friend, let me say to you, whose heart is aching, you need a friend like Jesus! He is just the Friend the widow needs. He is just the Friend every poor, anguished heart needs. He will have compassion on you and will bind up your wounded, bleeding heart, if you will only come to Him just as you are. He will receive you—without finding fault with you or punishing you—to His loving heart and say, *"Peace, be still"* (Mark 4:39). You can walk in the unclouded sunlight of His love from this time forward. Christ will be worth more to you than the whole world. He is just the Friend that you need, and I pray to God that you may know Him right now as your Savior and Friend.

THE MAN WHO WAS ROBBED

The next picture I want to show you to illustrate Christ's compassion is the parable of the Good Samaritan, found in the tenth chapter of Luke. A man is going down from Jerusalem to Jericho and falls among thieves. They take away his coat. They take his money. They strip him and leave him half dead. Imagine him wounded, bleeding, dying! And then a priest comes along and looks on the scene. His heart might have been touched, but he is not moved with compassion enough to help the poor man. He might have said, "Poor fellow!" but all he does is pass by on the other side.

After him comes a Levite, and perhaps he says, "Poor man!" but he is not moved with compassion to help him.

There are a great many people like that priest and Levite. When you meet a drunkard reeling in the street, do you just say, "Poor man"? Or, do you laugh when he stammers out some foolish thing? We are very much unlike the Son of God.

Finally, a Samaritan comes riding that way, and he looks on the man and has compassion on him. He gets off his animal, takes oil, pours it into the man's wounds, and binds them up. Then he takes the man out of the ditch, helpless as he is, places him on his own animal, brings him to an inn, and takes care of him!

That Good Samaritan represents your Christ and mine. He came into the world "*to*

14

seek and to save that which was lost" (Luke 19:10).

Young man, have you moved to the city and fallen in with bad companions? Have they taken you to places of depravity and left you bleeding and wounded? Come to the Son of God. He will have compassion on you. He will take you off the dunghill and transform you and lift you up into His kingdom, into the heights of His glory, if you will only let Him!

I do not care who you are. I do not care what your past life may have been. Jesus said to the poor woman who was caught in adultery, *"Neither do I condemn thee: go, and sin no more"* (John 8:11). He had compassion on her and He will have compassion on you. That man who was going down from Jerusalem to Jericho represents thousands in our large cities, and that Good Samaritan represents the Son of God. Young man, Jesus Christ has set His heart on saving you! Will you receive His love and compassion? Do not have such resentful thoughts about the Son of God. Do not think that He has come to condemn you. He has come to save you.

THE UNGRATEFUL SON

Now I want to draw you a picture of the Prodigal Son, whom we read about in fifteenth chapter of Luke. He is an ungrateful man, the most ungrateful wretch you have ever seen. He does not want to wait for his father to die before receiving his inheritance. He wants his share immediately, and so he says to his father, "Give me what belongs to me."

His good old father gives him his inheritance and off he goes. I can see him as he starts on his journey. He is full of pride, boastful and arrogant, setting out to see life, going off in style to some foreign country. How many people have done something similar, squandering all their money!

Yes, he is a popular young man as long as he has money. His friends last as long as his money does. "Glad to know you!" greets him everywhere. He always pays for the liquor and the cigars. Yes, he has plenty of "friends." What complete foolishness!

But when his money runs out, where are his friends? Oh, you who serve the Devil, you have a hard master! When the Prodigal's money was all gone, of course they laughed at him and called him a fool. That is exactly what he was.

What a blind, misguided young man he was. Just see what he lost. He lost his father's home, his source of food, his testimony, and every comfort. He lost his work; the only work he could get was a job feeding swine. This was an unlawful business for him. As a Jew, it was degrading for him to be feeding pigs, which were considered unclean animals. And that's just what the backslider is doing. He is in an unlawful business; he is in the Devil's pay. If you are in this situation, you are losing precious time as well as your Christian testimony. No one has any confidence in a backslider, for even the world despises such a person.

Yes, this young man lost his testimony. Look at him among the swine! I can imagine someone in that far country coming along, seeing him, and saying, "Look at that miserable, wretched, dirty, barefooted man taking care of swine!"

And the Prodigal exclaims, "Don't talk to me like that. Why, my father is a rich man and he has servants who are better dressed than you are."

"Don't tell me that!" says the other. "If you had a father like that, I know very well that he wouldn't acknowledge you."

No one would believe him. No one believes a backslider. He can talk about his fellowship with God, but nobody believes it. If you are a backslider, I pity you! You had better come home again.

Well, at last the poor Prodigal comes to himself and says, "I will leave this place and go to my father." So, he starts for home. Look at him as he goes along, pale and hungry, with his head down! His strength is exhausted. Perhaps his body is diseased and he is so shattered that no one would know him except his father.

But a loving heart is quick to detect the object of its love. The old man has often longed for his return. He has been up on the housetop many times, looking out to catch a glimpse of him. During many long nights he has wrestled with God in prayer so that his prodigal son might come back. Everything he has heard from that far country tells him that his boy is ruining his life as fast as he can. The old man has spent much time in prayer for him. At last, his faith begins to arise. "I believe God will send back my boy," he says.

One day, the old man sees the long lost boy a great distance away. He does not know him by his clothes but he recognizes his walk and says to himself, "Yes, that's my boy!"

I can see him hurrying down the stairs and rushing along the road. He is running! That is just like God. Many times in the Bible God is depicted as running. He is in a great hurry to meet the backslider. Yes, the old man is running. He sees his son from a great distance and he has compassion on him and hurries to meet him.

The boy wants to tell him his story—what he has done and where he has been—but the old man cannot stop to hear him. His heart is filled with compassion, and he lovingly holds his son close. The boy wants to go down into the kitchen with the servants, but the old man will not let him. No, he orders the servants to put shoes on his son's feet and a ring on his finger. He tells them to kill the fatted calf and to hold a celebration. The prodigal has come home; the wanderer has returned; and the old man rejoices over his return.

If you are a backslider, come home, and there will be joy in your heart and in the heart of God. May God bring you back today! Say, as the poor Prodigal did, "I will go to my Father," and on the authority of God I tell you that God will receive you. He will blot out your sins and restore you to His love. You will walk again in the light of His reconciled countenance.

CHRIST WEEPING OVER JERUSALEM

But look now at another picture that we find in the twenty-first chapter of Matthew. Jesus arrives at the Mount of Olives and sees the city of Jerusalem before Him. At a little distance is the temple, and He sees it in all its magnificence and glory. The people are shouting, "Hosanna to the son of David!" They are breaking off palm branches and taking off their coats and spreading them before Him. They are still shouting, "Hosanna to the son of David!" and bowing down before Him as He comes into the city and enters the temple.

But He forgets it all. Yes, He even forgets that He is about to face Calvary with all its sorrow. He forgets that He will have to wrestle in prayer at Gethsemane. The next day, He returns to the temple and the great heart of the Son of God is moved with compassion. He cries out in a loud voice concerning the city that He loves,

> *Jerusalem, Jerusalem, thou that killest the prophets, and stonest them which are sent unto thee, how often would I have gathered thy children together, even as a hen gathereth her chickens under her wings, and ye would not!   (Matt. 23:37)*

My friend, look at Him there, weeping over Jerusalem. What a wonderful city it might have been. How exalted to heaven it was! If the people had only known the day of their visitation and had received their King instead of rejecting Him, what a blessing He would have been to them. And, if you have fallen away from God, Jesus is weeping over you. He is crying to you to come to Him and to receive shelter and refuge from the storm that will sweep over this earth!

PETER'S DENIAL

Next, look at a picture of poor Peter from the twenty-sixth chapter of Matthew. Jesus has been arrested and Peter has denied the Lord and has sworn that he never knew Him. If Jesus ever needed sympathy, if He ever needed His disciples around Him, it was that night when the chief priests elders, and scribes were bringing false witnesses against Him so that He might be condemned to death. And there was Peter, one of His foremost disciples, swearing that he never knew Him. Jesus might have turned on Peter and said:

"Peter, is it true that you don't know Me? Is it true that you have forgotten how I healed your wife's mother when she was at the point of death? Is it true that you have forgotten how I caught you up when you were sinking in the sea? Is it true, Peter, that you have forgotten how you were with Me on the Mount of Transfiguration, when heaven and earth came together and you heard God's voice speaking from the clouds? Is it true that you have forgotten that mountain scene when you wanted to build the three tabernacles? Is it true, Peter, that you have forgotten Me?"

Yes, He might have taunted poor Peter in this way. But, instead of that, Luke's account of the incident says that Jesus just gives him one look of compassion that breaks his heart. *"And Peter went out, and wept bitterly"* (Luke 22:62).

SAUL, THE PERSECUTOR

Picture another scene that we read about in the ninth chapter of Acts. Look at Saul, that bold blasphemer and persecutor who is going to stamp out the early church and is breathing out threats and slaughter when Christ meets him on his way to Damascus. Jesus is still the same today. Pay close attention to what He says: *"Saul, Saul, why persecutest thou me?"* (Acts 9:4).

Jesus could have struck Saul to the earth with a look or a breath. But, instead of that, the heart of the Son of God is moved with compassion and He says, "Saul, why are you persecuting Me?"

Saul cries out in response, *"Who art thou, Lord?"* (v. 5).

And the Lord answers, *"I am Jesus whom thou persecutest. it is hard for thee to kick against the pricks"* (v. 5). In other words, He is saying, "It is hard for you to fight against such a loving friend, to contend against one who loves you as I do."

Proud, persecuting Saul falls down on his face and cries out, *"What wilt thou have me to do?"* (v. 6). The Lord tells him, and he does it immediately.

May the Lord have compassion on the unbeliever and skeptic and persecutor. If you are a persecutor, I want to ask you, Why persecute Jesus? He loves you, even though you are a sinner. He loves you, persecutor! You have never received anything but goodness and kindness and love from Him. My friend, is there any reason why you should hate Christ or why your heart should be turned against Him?

"WHY DON'T YOU LOVE JESUS?"

I remember a story about a teacher who told all her students to follow Jesus. She also told them how they could all become missionaries and go out to work for others. One day, one of the smallest came to her and said, "I asked a friend to come to class with me, and she said that she would like to come but that her father was an unbeliever." The young girl wanted to know what an unbeliever was, and the teacher explained it to her.

One day, when the child was on her way to school, this unbeliever was coming out of the post office with his letters in his hand, and she ran up to him and said, "Why don't you love Jesus?" At first he thought about pushing her aside, but the child pressed the question home again. "Why don't you love Jesus?"

If it had been a man, the unbeliever would have resented it, but he did not know how to respond to the child. With tears in her eyes, she asked him again, "Oh, please! Tell me, why don't you love Jesus?"

He went on to his office, but he felt as if every letter he opened read, "Why don't you love Jesus?" He attempted to write, but the same thing happened. Every letter seemed to ask him, "Why don't you love Jesus?" He threw down his pen in despair and left the office, but he could not get rid of the question. It was asked by a still, small voice within him. As he walked along, it seemed as if the very ground and the very heavens whispered to him, "Why don't you love Jesus?"

At last he went home, and there it seemed as if his own children asked him the question. Finally, he said to his wife, "I am going to go to bed early tonight," thinking that he would sleep it away. But when he laid his head on the pillow, it seemed as if the pillow whispered it to him. So, he got up about midnight and said, "I can find out where Christ contradicts Himself. I'll search it out and prove that He is a liar."

Well, he got up, turned to the gospel of John, and read on from the beginning until he came to the words,

> *God so loved the world, that he gave his only begotten Son, that whosoever believeth in him should not perish, but have everlasting life.* *(John 3:16)*

"What love!" he thought. At last, the old unbeliever's heart was stirred. He could find no reason for not loving Jesus, and so he went down on his knees and prayed. Before the sun rose, he was in the kingdom of God.

I will challenge anyone on the face of the earth to find any reason for not loving Christ. It is only here on earth that men think that they have a reason for not loving Him. In heaven, they know Him and they sing, *"Worthy is the Lamb that was slain"* (Rev. 5:12). Oh, if you knew Him, you would have no desire to find a reason for not loving Him! He is *"the chiefest among ten thousand"* and *"altogether lovely"* (Song 5:10, 16).

HOW DO I COME TO CHRIST?

I can imagine someone saying, "I would like very much to become a Christian, and I would like to know how I can come to Him and be saved."

Come to Him as a personal Friend. Christ is just as frequently near, as personally present to me, as any other living person. For years, I have made this a rule: when I have any troubles, trials, and heartaches, I go to Him with them. When I need counsel, I go to Him just as if I could talk with Him face to face.

Twenty years ago, God met me and took me to His heart. And I would rather give up my life right now than give up Christ or leave Him, or be without Jesus and have no one to bear my burdens or tell my sorrows to. He is worth more than the whole world. And, right now, He will have compassion on you as He had on me. I tried for weeks to find a way to Him. Finally, I just went and laid my burden on Him, and then He revealed Himself to me. And, ever since, I have found Him to be a true and sympathizing Friend, just the Friend you need. Go right straight to Him! You do not need to go to this person or that person, to this church or that church. Jesus said, *"I am the way, the truth, and the life"* (John 14:6).

THE HEART OF COMPASSION

There is no name as dear to Americans as that of Abraham Lincoln. Do you want to know the reason why? He was a man of compassion. He was very gentle and was noted for his heart of sympathy for the downtrodden and the poor. He had compassion on anyone who came to him with a sad story, no matter how far down the person was in the scale of society. He always took an interest in the poor.

There was a time in our history when we thought he had too much compassion. During the Civil War, many of our soldiers did not understand army discipline, and a great many were not true to army regulations. They intended to be, but they did not understand them. As a result, many men got into serious trouble and were court-martialed and condemned to be shot. But Abraham Lincoln would always pardon them. After a while, the nation rose up against him and said that he was too merciful. Ultimately, they got him to order that if a man was court-martialed, he must be shot. There would be no more reprieves.

A few weeks after this, news came that a young soldier had been sleeping at his post. He was court-martialed and condemned to be shot.

The boy wrote to his mother, "I do not want you to think I do not love my country, but it came about in this way: My comrade was sick, and I went out on picket for him. The next night he should have come, but because he was still sick I went out for him again, and without intending it, I fell asleep. I did not intend to be disloyal."

It was a very touching letter. His mother and father said there was no chance for him. There were to be no more reprieves. But there was a little girl in that home, and she knew that Abraham Lincoln had a little boy that he loved very much. And she thought that if Abraham Lincoln knew how much her father and mother loved her brother, he would never allow him to be shot. So, she took the train to go and plead for her brother.

When she got to the president's mansion, the difficulty arose as to how she was to get past the sentinel. She told him her story and the tears ran down his cheeks and he let her pass. But the next problem was how to get past the secretary and the other officials. However, she succeeded in getting, unobstructed, into Lincoln's private room, and there she saw the senators and cabinet members, busy with state affairs.

The president saw the child. He called her to him and said, "My child, what can I do for you?" She told him her story. The big tears rolled down his cheeks. He was a father, and his heart was full; he could not stand it. He treated the girl with kindness, reprieved the boy, gave him thirty days of furlough, and sent him home to see his mother. His heart was full of compassion.

Let me tell you, Christ has more compassion than any man. You are condemned to die for your sins. But if you go to Him, He will say, *"Loose him, and let him go"* (John 11:44). He will rebuke Satan. Go to Him as that little girl went to the president and tell Him everything. Keep nothing from Him, and He will say, *"Go in peace"* (Mark 5:34).

THE TOUCH OF COMPASSION

Have you ever felt the touch of the hand of Jesus? If so, you will recognize it again, for there is love in it.

There is another story told in connection with the Civil War of a mother who received a message that her boy was mortally wounded. She went down to the front, for she knew that the soldiers who had been told to watch the sick and wounded could not watch her boy as she could.

So she went to the doctor and said, "Would you like me to take care of my boy?" The doctor said, "We have just let him go to sleep. If you go to him, the surprise will be so great that it might be dangerous to him. He is in a very critical state. I will break the news to him gradually."

"But," said the mother, "he may never wake up. I would so dearly like to see him."

Finally, the doctor said, "You can see him, but if you wake him up and he dies, it will be your fault."

"Well," she said, "I will not wake him up if I may just go to his cot and see him."

She went to the side of his cot. Her eyes had longed to see him. As she gazed on him, she could not keep her hand off that pale forehead, and she laid it gently there. There was love and sympathy in that hand, and the moment the sleeping boy felt it, he said, "Oh, mother, have you come?"

He knew there was sympathy and affection in the touch of that hand. And if you will let Jesus reach out His hand and touch your heart, you too will find that there is sympathy and love in it. It is the prayer of my heart that everyone who is lost may be saved and come to the arms of our blessed Savior!

Chapter 2

What Salvation Is

I hope that your own heart has been moved
by reading about the compassion Christ
has for you and that you now want to come
to Him. I believe that this very moment is a
crisis in the history of a great many people
around the world. Thousands are just hesitat-
ing and wavering. They are almost persuaded
to commit their lives to Christ. Many are saying to themselves, "I don't want to be without
Christ. I want to be saved today."

I have just one goal, and that is to answer
the question that many people are asking:
"What must I do to be saved?" (Acts 16:30).
This is the first question that is asked by every
person who is honestly and truly inquiring
about the way of salvation. And, God helping
me, I will try to make it plain to you.

BELIEVING

If I say to you, "Believe on the Lord Jesus Christ," you may reply, "Oh, 'believe'! I have heard that word until I am sick and tired of it. Almost every week I hear it in church or at a prayer meeting." You have heard it over and over again. But you need to know *how* to believe—what it is to believe.

Some of you are saying, "We all believe that Christ came into the world to seek and to save the lost, and that he who believes will be saved." That's fine, but even the devils believe and are not saved. Yes, *"the devils also believe, and tremble"* (James 2:19). You must believe *on* the Lord Jesus Christ and not merely *about* Him, and then you will know what salvation is.

RECEIVING

Instead of the word *believe,* let's take another word that means the same thing: *receive.* Perhaps you'll grasp this concept better.

> *He came unto his own, and his own received him not. But as many as received him, to them gave he power to become the sons of God, even to them that believe on his name.* (John 1:11–12)

Bear in mind that the Scripture says, *"received him."* That's the key. It does not say,

"As many as received a doctrine or a belief," but, *"As many as received him."* It is a Person we must receive.

It has been my experience that we all want to have the power before we receive Christ. That is, we want to *feel* that we are in Christ before we will receive Him. But we cannot love God and feel His presence until we have received Him into our hearts.

Suppose that you are playing catch with your son and he throws the ball to you. Well, you must catch the ball before you can throw it back again. The real meaning of the word *believe* is "receive." You must receive Christ as your own. I don't know any verse in the Bible that God has made a blessing to more people than John 1:12: *"But as many as received him, to them gave he power."*

In addition, I don't know of any better illustration of salvation that I could give you than the example of marriage. The Bible uses it, and if God uses it in His Word, why shouldn't I? In the Old Testament, God said, *"I am married unto you"* (Jer. 3:14). Jesus Himself used the illustration when He spoke of the bride in John 3:29. Paul used it in his epistles, as in Romans 7:4, as an illustration of the union between Christ and His church.

Now, this is an example that everyone can understand; there is no one who does not know what it means. When a man proposes to a woman, she must do one of two things—receive him or reject him. In the same way, everyone reading this book must do one of two things—receive Christ or reject Him. If you receive Him, that is all you have to do. He has promised you power to become a child of God.

A few years ago, I heard about a saleswoman in Chicago. One day she could not have bought a dollar's worth of anything, and the next day she could go and buy a thousand dollars' worth of whatever she wanted. What made the difference? Why, she had married a rich husband, that was all. She had received him and, of course, all that he owned had become hers. And so, you can have power if you will only receive Christ. Remember, you can have no power without Him. You will fail, and fail constantly, until you receive Him into your heart. And I have the authority of Scripture to say that Christ will receive every person who will only come to Him. *"All that the Father giveth me shall come to me; and him that cometh to me I will in no wise cast out"* (John 6:37).

Rebekah and Isaac

In Genesis 24 we read how Abraham sent his servant Eliezer on a long journey to get a wife for his son, Isaac. When Eliezer found Rebekah, he wanted to return immediately with the young bride. However, her mother and brother said, "No, she must wait awhile." But Eliezer was determined to go. Therefore, they said, "We will ask the girl." When Rebekah appeared, they asked her, "Will you go with this man?"

That was a crisis in her life. She could have said no. Undoubtedly, it was a strain on her; it would, of course, have been a struggle. She had to give up her parents, her home, her friends, all that she loved, and go with this stranger. But look at her reply! She said, "I will go."

I have come to get a bride for my Master. I can tell you one thing that Eliezer could not tell Rebekah. He could not say, "Isaac loves you," because Isaac had never seen his bride. But I can say, "My Master loves you! He gave Himself for you." Yes, that is love!

But, bear in mind, my friend, that the moment Rebekah made up her mind to accept Isaac, he became everything to her, so that she did not feel she was giving up anything for him. What a mistake some people make! They say, "I'd become a Christian if I didn't have to give up so much." Just turn it around and look at it the other way. You don't have to give up anything; you simply have to receive. And when you have received Christ, everything else vanishes pretty quickly. When Christ fills you, you will no longer feel that these things are worth a thought

When a woman marries a man, it is generally love that prompts her. If a woman really loves a man, is she thinking of how much she will have to give up? No, that wouldn't be love. Love doesn't feed on itself. It feeds on the person who is loved. So, my friend, it is not by looking at what you will have to give up, but by looking at what you will receive, that you will be enabled to accept the Savior.

What Will Christ Do for You?

What is Jesus willing to do and to be for you, if you will have Him? Won't you be made an heir of heaven, a joint-heir with Christ (Rom. 8:17)? Won't you reign with Him forever and ever (Rev. 22:5)? Won't you belong to Him? Won't you be with Him and become like Him? Think, then, of what He is and of what He gives. You don't need to trouble yourself about what you will have to give up. Receive Him, and all these things will appear utterly insignificant.

I used to think about what I would have to give up. I dearly loved many of the pleasures of this world. But now, I'd just as soon go out into the street and eat dirt as do those things. God doesn't say, "Give up this and that." He says, "Here is the Son of My heart—receive Him." When you do receive Him, everything else goes. Stop talking about giving up things. Let Christ save you, and all these things will be worthless to you.

Have you ever known a man or woman who regretted receiving Him? No one ever regretted receiving Christ, but I have heard of thousands who have been followers of the Devil and have regretted it bitterly. And I notice that it is always the most faithful followers of the Devil who end up regretting it most.

My friend, accept my advice and receive Jesus now. Remember, He is the Gift of God and is offered to whoever will take Him. You belong to that group, don't you? Just take Him. That's the first thing you have to do. When you go to cut down a tree, you don't take the ax and begin to chop down the branches. No, you begin right down at the root. In the same way, you must begin at the foundation. You must take Christ, and then you will receive power to resist the world, the flesh, and the Devil.

Ruth and Orpah

Another illustration of receiving Christ may be found in the story of Ruth and Orpah

from the book of Ruth. Many people are like
these two young widows who were living in the
mountains of Moab. A crisis had come into
their lives. They had both lost their husbands.
I imagine that they had often visited the
graves of their dear ones. They probably had
planted a few flowers there and watered them
with their tears.

But now, Naomi, their mother-in-law, has
resolved to return to her own country. They
decide to travel a small part of the journey
with her. Down in the valley, they each embrace Naomi and give her a farewell kiss. It is
a sad parting, but then the decisive moment
comes. Both young widows say they will go
with her. However, Naomi warns them of the
difficulties and trials that might await them,
and so Orpah says, "I will go back to my people." But Ruth cannot leave her mother-in-law
and says she wants to go with her.

Orpah turns back alone. I can see her on
the top of the hill. She stops and turns around
for a last look. And Naomi says to Ruth, "See,
your sister-in-law has gone back to her people
and to her gods. Go back with your sister-in-
law."

What does Ruth answer?

*Entreat me not to leave thee, or to return
from following after thee: for whither*

*thou goest, I will go; and where thou
lodgest, I will lodge: thy people shall be
my people, and thy God my God.*

(Ruth 1:16)

Orpah loved Naomi, but not enough to
leave everything for her. Ruth loved her
mother-in-law so much that to leave her people
seemed nothing to her. Oh, may God draw out
your heart, so that you may leave all and follow Him!

We never hear any more about Orpah; the
curtain falls on her life. Perhaps she died, way
up in the mountains of Moab, without God and
without hope. But how different it was with
Ruth! She became famous in history. She is one
of the few women whose names have remained
on the honor roll of the ages, and she was
brought into the royal line of heaven. I have an
idea that God blessed her for that decision. And
He will bless you if you decide in a similar man-
ner. Will you say, as Ruth did, "I will follow
you" and, "Your God will be my God"? Are you
a Ruth? If so, the Master is calling.

"Who Will Receive Him Now?"

Once, after a service in Dublin, Ireland, I
was speaking to a lady in the inquiry room—a
certain room that is set aside for people who

have additional questions about salvation—when I noticed a young gentleman walking up and down in front of the door. I went forward and asked, "Are you a Christian?" He was angry, and he turned on his heel and left.

The following Sunday night, I was preaching about receiving, and I asked the question, "Who will receive Him now?" The same young man, who was a businessman in that city, was present, and the question sank into his heart. The next day, he came to visit me and said, "Do you remember me?"

"No, I don't."

"Do you remember the young man who answered you so rudely the other night?"

"Yes."

"Well, I've come to tell you I am saved."

"How did it happen?"

"Why, I was listening to your sermon last night, and when you asked, 'Who will receive Him now?' God put it into my heart to say, 'I will.' And He has opened my eyes to see His Son now."

I don't know why you shouldn't do the same thing that young man did. If you are ever going to be saved, why not now?

A Free Gift

But there is another point you must remember. Salvation is a free gift, and it is a free gift for you. Can you buy it? No, it is a free gift, presented to whoever will receive it.

Suppose I were to say, "I will give my Bible to whoever wants it." What do you have to do? Why, nothing, except take it. But then, suppose that a man comes up to me and says, "I'd like that Bible very much."

"Well, didn't I say I would give it to 'whoever'?"

"Yes, but I'd like you to mention my name specifically."

"Well, here is the Bible."

The man continues eyeing the Bible and saying, "I'd like to have that Bible, but I'd like to give you something for it. I don't want to take it for nothing."

"My friend, I am not here to sell Bibles. Take it, if you want it."

"Well, I do want it. However, I'd like to give you something for it. Let me pay you a small amount for it, even though it's certainly worth more than that."

Suppose that I accept his money. Now the man takes the Bible and marches home with it. His wife asks, "Where did you get that Bible?"

"Oh, I bought it."

Note the point: when he gave the money, it ceased to be a gift. It is the same way with salvation. If you were to pay even a small amount for it, it would not be a gift.

TRUSTING

Now, let's take another word that may help you to understand salvation. I have been speaking of the word *receive.* The next word I want to call to your attention is *trust.* Many people can grasp that concept when they cannot comprehend *believe* or *receive.*

You know what it is to trust. If it were not for trust, there would be a terrible commotion in your life. If you could not trust that your roof was secure, you would get out of your house pretty quickly. If you could not trust your chair to support you, how long would you sit in it? Yet, you confidently trust in these things every day. God wants you to trust Him in the same way. He is not looking for a miraculous kind of trust or faith. He is looking for simple trust. However, the object of your trust is different than what I have just been describing. Instead of trusting in these earthly things or in *"an arm of flesh"* (2 Chron. 32:8), He asks you to trust in the Son of God.

The Uselessness of Trying

Mankind is always trying to do something to earn salvation. This miserable word *try* is keeping thousands out of heaven. When I hear people speak of "trying," I generally tell them that that is the way down to death and hell. I believe that more souls are lost through "trying" than through any other way.

Perhaps you have often tried and failed. As long as you keep trying, you will fail. Drop that word, then, and take trust as your sure foothold for eternity. *"Though he slay me, yet will I trust in him"* (Job 13:15). That is the right kind of trust. I pray to God that you will say, "I will trust Him right now." Have you ever heard of anyone who went to hell trusting in Jesus? I never have. This very day, if you commit yourself to Him, the battle will be over.

Perhaps you are complaining that you don't *feel* any better. Well, remember, a child must be born before it can be taught. In the same way, we cannot learn about God until we receive Him. We must be born—born again, have the new birth—before we can feel. Christ must be *"in* [us], *the hope of glory"* (Col. 1:27). How can He be in us if we don't receive Him and trust Him?

Salvation in the Present Tense

Another verse that has been a help to many people, and on which I rest my own salvation, is John 5:24. I trust that God will write it on your heart and burn it down into your soul. *"Verily, verily, I say unto you, He that heareth my word, and believeth on him that sent me, hath everlasting life."* Thank God for that word *hath!*

I was talking with a few men in the inquiry room after a service one night. They said that they could not find peace, and so I asked them, "Do you believe the Bible?"

"Yes, sir," they said.

"I think I will prove that you don't. Turn to John 5:24."

They turned to it.

"Read the verse."

"'He that heareth my word'—"

"Do you believe that?"

"Yes, sir."

"'And believeth on him that sent me'—do you believe God sent Jesus?"

"Yes."

"Well, read on."

"'Hath everlasting life.'"

"Do you believe you have everlasting life?"

"No, we don't."

"Oh, I thought you believed the Bible! What right do you have to cut a verse in two and say that you believe one half but not the other? It plainly says that he who believes *'hath everlasting life, and shall not come into condemnation; but is passed from death unto life.'* If you believe God's words, you can say, 'I have passed from darkness into light.' Just by resting on that one little word, *hath,* in the present tense, you can have assurance now. You don't need to wait until you die or until the great Day of Judgment to find out if you have eternal life."

Take the Water of Life

A lady in Glasgow, Scotland, came to me and said, "Mr. Moody, you are always saying, 'Take, take!' Is there any place in the Bible where it says *take,* or is it only a word you use? I have been looking for it in the Bible, but I cannot find it."

"Why," I said, "the Bible is sealed with it. It is almost the last word in the Bible. Revelation 22:17 says, *'And the Spirit and the bride say, Come. And let him that heareth say, Come. And let him that is athirst come. And whosoever will, let him take the water of life freely.'"*

"I never saw that before," she said. "Is that all I have to do?"

"Yes, the Bible says so."

And she took the Water of Life, right there. God says, *"Let him take."* Who can stop us if God says it? All the devils in hell cannot hinder a poor soul from taking if God says

"Take." My friend, are you going to take Christ today? Are you going to finish this book without being able to say, "Christ is my Savior. God is my Father Heaven is my home"?

HAVING LIFE NOW

A lady came to my house one evening, very concerned about her soul. However, after we had talked for a while, she left without finding peace. She came another time and I asked her, "What is the trouble?"

"I haven't got peace."

I opened my Bible and showed her John 3:36. *"He that believeth on the Son hath everlasting life."* I just emphasized that little word *hath*. I also turned to John 5:24 and John 6:47. All these verses are words spoken by Jesus and are linked to believing on the Son. After we had talked for some time, she looked in my face earnestly and said, "I've got it!" and went away rejoicing in the Savior's love.

The word *hath* also occurs in Isaiah 53:6: *"All we like sheep have gone astray...and the LORD hath laid on him the iniquity of us all."* If you seek life, you can have it now. Our sins have been laid on Christ, and God is not going to demand payment twice. *"Who his own self bare our sins in his own body on the tree"* (1 Pet. 2:24).

What Salvation Is

The Debt Is Fully Paid

Suppose that I borrow a thousand dollars from a man and then cannot repay him. I am in danger of being sued. But then, suppose that a friend of mine hears about it and says, "I don't want to see Moody taken to court." So he pays the debt for me and gets the receipt. When I see the receipt, I know that I am free. Now, what if the man finds out that I didn't pay it myself and gets me hauled off to court anyway? He says that I must pay it personally. I show the receipt.

"Why," says the judge, "the debt is paid."

The man says, "Moody didn t pay it."

Would any judge in the land support him? No. The debt has been paid and cannot be demanded again. And if man doesn't ask for payment twice, will God? No, certainly not! The case is this: The debt has been paid. Our sins have been atoned for. Christ Himself has redeemed us, not with perishable things such as silver and gold, but with His precious blood. Therefore, we are free!

But, remember, although salvation is free to us, it cost God a great deal to redeem us. He had an only Son, and He gave Him up freely for us. What a wonderful gift! Yet, if you make light of such remarkable salvation, how can you escape the damnation of hell? *"How shall*

we escape, if we neglect so great salvation?"
(Heb. 2:3).

The Great Question

Now, one question: What are you going to do with Christ? You have to settle that question. You may get angry about it, like a man who marched out of a church a short time ago, saying, "What right has that man to ask such a question?" But it is true—you must settle the question. We read in Luke 23 that Pontius Pilate wanted to shirk the responsibility and that is why he sent Jesus to Herod. However, he was still forced into a decision. Matthew's gospel tells us that when the Jews pressured Pilate to decide, he washed his hands and said that he was *"innocent of the blood of this just person"* (Matt. 27:24). But did that take away his guilt? No.

An angel may be near you, listening to what you say. If you say decisively, "I will receive Him. I will delay no longer," the angel will wing his way right up to the pearly gates and tell the news that another sinner has been saved. A new song will ring through the courts of heaven because a sinner has repented. God will issue the command to write down your name in the Book of Life and to get rooms ready for you in the New Jerusalem, where we all will be soon.

What Salvation Is

Guilty, but Safe

Once, in another country, a man was being tried for a crime, the punishment of which was death. The witnesses came in, one by one, and testified to his guilt, but he was quite calm and unmoved. The judge and the jury were quite surprised at his indifference. They could not understand how he could take such a serious matter so calmly. When the jury withdrew to deliberate, it did not take them many minutes to decide on a guilty verdict. And when the judge was passing the sentence of death on the criminal, he told him how surprised he was that he could be so unmoved at the prospect of death.

When the judge had finished, the man put his hand in his inside coat pocket, pulled out a document, and walked out of the courtroom a free man. It was a pardon from his king, which he had had in his pocket the whole time. That was how he could be so calm! The king had instructed him to allow the trial to proceed and to produce the pardon only when he was condemned. It is no wonder, then, that he was indifferent regarding the result of the trial. Similarly, we who believe in Christ will not come into judgment. We have a pardon from the Great King, and it is sealed with the blood of His Son.

You Will Live Forever

There's Help for You

After the Great Chicago Fire took place, a great many things were sent to the city from all parts of the world. The boxes they came in were labeled, "For the people who lost everything in the fire." All a person had to do was to prove that his belongings had been burned, and then he got a share. In the same way, you only have to prove that you are a poor, miserable sinner, and there's help for you. As long as a person who is ruined and lost clings to the word *try,* he has no hope. But if he will stop trying to come to God in his own strength, recognizing it as a useless and self-justifying attempt, then Christ will save him. The law condemns us, but Christ saves us.

He'll Take You As You Are

The superintendent of a Sunday school in Edinburgh, Scotland, was walking down the street one night when he met a policeman who was leading a little boy by the hand. The boy was crying bitterly. The man stopped and asked the policeman what was the matter with the boy.

"Oh," said the officer, "he is lost."

The superintendent asked if he could get a clearer look at him. They went to a street light and held the little fellow up to it. Immediately, the boy recognized his superintendent and flew into his arms. The gentleman took him from the policeman, and the boy was comforted. The law has us, but if we flee into Jesus' arms, we are safe.

A friend of mine told me about a poor Scottish girl who was very concerned about her soul. He told her to read Isaiah 53. She replied, "I canna read and I canna pray. Jesus, take me as I am!"

That was the true way, and Jesus took her just as she was. Let Him take you today, just as you are, and He will receive you into His arms.

Don't Trust in Your Feelings

One night, when I was preaching in Philadelphia, there was a young lady sitting right by the side of the pulpit. Her eyes were riveted on me as if she were drinking in every word. It is precious to preach to people like that. They generally receive spiritual help, even if the sermon is poor.

I began to wonder about her, and after I had finished talking, I went and spoke to her.

"Are you a Christian?" I asked.

"No, I wish I was. I have been seeking Jesus for three years."

"There must be some mistake."

She looked at me with a puzzled expression and said, "Don't you believe me?"

"Well, no doubt you *thought* you were seeking Jesus. But it doesn't take an anxious sinner three years to meet a concerned and compassionate Savior."

"What am I to do, then?"

"The problem is that you are trying to do something. You must just believe on the Lord Jesus Christ."

"Oh, I am sick and tired of hearing 'Believe, believe believe!' I don't know what it means."

"Well," I said, "we'll change the word. Take the word *trust*."

"If I say I'll trust Him, will He save me?"

"No, I didn't say that. You may *say* a thousand things, but if you *do* trust Him, He will save you."

"Well," she said, "I do trust Him. But," she added in the same breath, "I don't feel any better."

"Ah, I've got it now! For three years you've been looking for feelings, instead of for Jesus. Faith is up above, not down here."

People are often looking for feelings. If you were to put together a new translation of the Bible, and if those responsible for translating it were to put in the word *feelings* instead of *faith,* what a demand there would be for that Bible! But if you were to look from Genesis to

Revelation, you could not find any Scripture that says that feelings are connected with salvation. We must rise above feelings.

"Feelings" is the last plank that the Devil sticks out just as your feet are getting on the Rock of Ages. He sees the poor, trembling sinner just about to find his way to the Savior, and so he shoves out this plank, and the poor sinner thinks, "I'm all right now." Perhaps some sermon you hear stirs you, but then you feel all right when you get on this plank and you don't do anything about it. Six months after, perhaps, you are dying, and the Devil comes along when you think you're quite safe. "Ah," he tells you, "that was my work. I made you feel good." What will you do then? Oh, take your stand on God's Word, and then you cannot fail! His Word has been tried for six thousand years, and it has never failed.

Now, to resume my story, I said to the young lady in Philadelphia, "You've been relying on your feelings, but you cannot control how you feel. Have no more to do with feelings. Instead, like Job, say, *'Though he slay me, yet will I trust in him'*" (Job 13:15).

She looked at me for a few minutes, and then, stretching out her hand to take mine, she said, "Mr. Moody, I trust the Lord Jesus Christ to save my soul tonight." Then she went to the elders of the church and said the same thing. As she left the church, she met one of the church officers and, shaking his hand, said again, "I trust the Lord Jesus to save my soul."

The next night she was right in front of me again. I will never forget her beaming face. The light of eternity was shining in her eyes! Then she went into the inquiry room. I wondered what she was going there for, but when I got there, I found her with her arms around a lady friend, saying, "You only need to trust Him! This is what I have discovered."

From that night, she was one of the best workers in the inquiry room. Whenever I came across a difficult case, I got her to speak to the person, and she was sure to help him.

Worthy of Acceptance

You can certainly trust God today. You must have a very poor opinion of God if you cannot trust Him. You only have to come to Him and receive Him, trust Him. What more can you do, and what less can you do, than trust Him? Is He not worthy of it? Christ is standing at the door of your heart, knocking. Go to a quiet place and think of this passage of Scripture:

Behold, I stand at the door, and knock:
if any man hear my voice, and open the

> door, *I will come in to him, and will sup*
> *with him, and he with me.* (Rev. 3:20)

Will you pull back the bolts on the door
and say, "Blessed Savior, come in"? I earnestly
pray to God that you will do this.

Chapter 3

What Is the Gospel?

In the last chapter, I described the meaning of the words *receive* and *trust*. Now I want to explain the meaning of the word *Gospel*. Most of us have heard this word ever since we were children. Yet there is no word in the English language that is as little understood as this one. Many people receive the salvation and blessings of the Gospel a long time before they really know what it means.

Gospel means "good tidings." It would do us good from time to time to get a dictionary and hunt up the meaning of some of the words we use so often, some of these Bible words. It would change our ideas.

You would be very joyful today if you really believed that the Gospel is good news. When someone receives a letter that brings good news, you know it immediately, because his face lights up when he reads it. You can see he truly believes it. If it is really good news—if, for example, it brings him the news that a long lost son is coming home—and if his wife is sitting near him, he shows the letter to her. He wants her to know about it, too. He does not wait for her to ask for it. He does not wait until a later time to show it to her. And, when I preach, if I am near enough to look into the eyes of those who really believe the Gospel, I see their faces light up, and they look interested. But those who do not believe the Gospel put on a long face and look as if I had brought them a death warrant or invited them to a funeral.

GOOD NEWS OF GREAT JOY

The Gospel is *"good tidings of great joy"* (Luke 2:10). This is the message that the angels brought to the shepherds when they announced that the Christ had been born.

> *Behold, I bring you good tidings of great joy, which shall be to all people. For unto you is born this day in the city of David a Saviour, which is Christ the Lord.* (Luke 2:10–11)

No better news ever came out of heaven, no better news ever fell upon the ears of the family of man, than the Gospel. After the angels had gone away, the shepherds said,

*Let us now go even unto Bethlehem, and
see this thing which is come to pass,
which the Lord hath made known unto
us.* (Luke 2:15)

The shepherds believed the message. They
were full of joy and left immediately for Bethlehem.

Now, if those shepherds had been like a
great many people today, they would have said,
"We do not believe it is good news. It is all excitement. Those angels just want to stir up a
revival. They are trying to excite us. Don't believe them!"

That is what Satan is saying now. "Don't
believe that the Gospel is good news." He knows
that the moment a person believes good news,
he just receives it. Never, in all my life, have I
seen anyone who did not like good news. And
every person who is under the power of the
Devil does not believe that the Gospel is good
news. The moment you are out from under his
power and influence, then you believe it. I pray
to God that the Gospel may sink deep into your
heart, and that you may believe it and be saved!

RECONCILIATION WITH GOD

The Gospel is the best news that ever
came to this sin-cursed earth. We are dead in

trespasses and sins, but God wants us to be reconciled to Him. It is a Gospel of reconciliation, and God is calling to mankind from the heights of glory, "I am reconciled. Now you be reconciled!"

I have glorious news to tell you. Through Christ's substitutionary death on the cross, God is reconciled, and He implores His subjects to be reconciled to Him. The great apostle says, *"We pray you in Christ's stead, be ye reconciled to God"* (2 Cor. 5:20). The moment a person believes the Gospel, he unclenches his rebellious fist, and the unequal controversy is over. A light from Calvary crosses his path, and he can walk in unclouded sunshine, if he will. And it is your privilege right now to walk in unclouded sunshine, if you will. What brought darkness into the world? Darkness came because of sin, and the person who does not believe the Gospel is blinded by the god of this world:

> *In whom the god of this world hath blinded the minds of them which believe not, lest the light of the glorious gospel of Christ, who is the image of God, should shine unto them.* (2 Cor. 4:4)

I like the Gospel because it is the very best news I have ever heard. The reason I like to preach it is because it has done me so much good. A person cannot preach the Gospel until he believes it himself. He must know it down deep in his own heart before he can tell it to others—and even then he tells it only very poorly at best. We are very poor ambassadors and messengers. But, never mind the messenger, take hold of the message. That is what you need. If a boy brought me good news today, I would not care what the boy looked like. I would not care what his skin color was or whether he was educated or uneducated. The message is what would do me good. A great many people look at the messenger instead of the message. Never mind the messenger! My friend, get hold of the message today. The Gospel is what saves, and it is my prayer that you may believe the Gospel now.

YOUR SINS FORGIVEN

In the fifteenth chapter of 1 Corinthians, the apostle Paul explained what the Gospel is. He began by writing, *"I declare unto you the gospel"* (v. 1). And the first thing he stated in his declaration to these Corinthians was this: *"Christ died for our sins according to the scriptures"* (v. 3). That was the old-fashioned Gospel. I hope we will never get away from it. I don't want anything but that old, old story.

What Is the Gospel?

Some people have itching ears for something new. Bear in mind that there is no new Gospel. Christ died for our sins. If He did not, how are we going to get rid of them? Would you insult the Almighty by offering your own frail efforts to atone for sin? If Christ did not die for our sins, what is going to become of our souls?

The apostle Paul then goes on to explain that Christ rose again. He burst the bonds of death. Death could not hold Him. I can imagine that, if we could have been there when they laid Jesus in Joseph's sepulcher, we would have seen Death sitting over that sepulcher, saying, "I have Him. He is my victim. He said that He was the resurrection and the life. Now I have Him in my cold embrace. Look at Him! He has had to pay tribute to me. Some thought He was never going to die. Some thought I would not get Him. But He is mine."

Yet, look what happened! The glorious morning came, and the Son of Man broke apart the bonds of death and came out of the sepulcher. We do not worship a dead God but a Savior who still lives. He rose from the grave! Then the disciples saw Him ascend to heaven. He went up and took His seat at the right hand of God (Mark 16:19).

And He will return to earth again, for He said, *"I will come again"* (John 14:3). The

Gospel, therefore, consists of five things: Christ's death, burial, resurrection, ascension, and coming again. Thanks be to God, He is coming back soon! He will come and take the kingdom. He will swing His scepter from the rivers to the ends of the earth. In a little while, He will rule and reign. Let us lift up our heads and rejoice that the time of our redemption is drawing near.

Let us get back to the simple Gospel: Christ died for our sins. We must know Christ at Calvary first, as our Redeemer, as our Substitute. The moment we accept Him as our Redeemer, we become partakers of the Gospel. The moment we believe in the Lord Jesus Christ as our Substitute—at that moment—we receive light and peace. Some people say, "Oh, the important thing is not Christ's death, but His life. Do not preach so much about the death of Christ. Preach about His life."

My friend, that never will save anyone. Paul said, *"I declare unto you the gospel...Christ died"*—not Christ lived—*"for our sins"* (1 Cor. 15:1, 3). *"Who his own self bare our sins in his own body on the tree"* (1 Pet. 2:24). Now, when I accept Christ as my Savior, as my Substitute, then I am *"justified from all things, from which [I] could not be justified by the law of Moses"* (Acts 13:39).

What Is the Gospel?

YOUR WORST ENEMIES REMOVED

I like the Gospel because it has removed from my path the worst enemies I ever had: death, sin, and judgment.

Free from Death

My mind goes back twenty years to the time before I was converted. I remember how dark things sometimes used to seem when I thought of the future. I knew that death would eventually come—and what a terrible enemy it seemed! I was brought up in a little village in New England. It was the custom there, when a person was buried, to toll out the age of the deceased. I used to count the strokes of the bell. There was never a time when death entered that village and tore away one of the inhabitants that I did not count the tolling of the bell. Sometimes it would be way up between seventy and eighty, beyond the years allotted to man, and it seemed to me that the person had been living on borrowed time. Sometimes it would be clear down in the teens, and death would take away someone my own age. It used to make a solemn impression on me. I used to be a great coward.

When it comes to death, some people say, "I do not fear it." Well, I feared it I felt terribly afraid when I thought of the cold hand of Death feeling for the cords of life and of being launched into eternity, into an unknown world. I used to have terrifying thoughts about God, but they are all gone now. Death has lost its sting. As I go through the world, I can shout, when the bell is tolling, *"O death, where is thy sting?"* (1 Cor. 15:55). And I hear a voice echoing back from Calvary, saying, "It is buried in the heart of the Son of God."

Jesus Christ robbed death of its sting. He took the sting of death into His own heart. If you take a wasp and remove the sting from it, you will not be afraid of it any more than you would be afraid of a little fly. The sting has been taken out. And you do not need to be afraid of death if you are in Christ. Christ died for your sin. The penalty, or the wages, of sin is death (Rom. 6:23). Christ received the penalty on Calvary; therefore, there is no condemnation for you. All that death can get now is the "old Adam" or *"body of sin"* (Rom. 6:6) as Paul called it. I do not mind the fact that I will soon get rid of it. I will get a better body, a resurrected body, a glorified body, a body much better than this. Yes, my friend, *"to die,"* says the apostle, *"is gain"* (Phil. 1:21). If a man is in Christ, let death come!

Suppose that Death should come stealing up to me and lay his cold, icy hand upon my heart, and it should cease to beat. I would rise to another world and be in the presence of the King. I would be absent from the body but present with the Lord (2 Cor. 5:8). That is not bad news. There is no use in trying to conceal it; the thought of death is an enemy to a person's peace. What a glorious thought, then, to think that when you die you will sink into the arms of Jesus, and that He will carry you away to the world of light beyond. A little while longer here, a few more tears, and then you can gain an unbroken rest in the world of light beyond! When the Gospel turns that enemy into a friend, you can even rejoice in death.

Years ago, I used to go and look into the cold, silent grave and think of that terrible hour when I would have to be laid down in the grave, and this body would be eaten up with worms. But, now, the grave has lost its terror and gloom for me. I can go and look down into the grave and shout over it, *"O grave, where is thy victory?"* (1 Cor. 15:55). And I also hear a voice coming up from the grave. It is the shout of the Conqueror, of Him who has been down in the grave and has measured the depth of it. It is the shout of my Lord and Savior: *"Because I live, ye shall live also"* (John 14:19).

Yes, the grave has lost its victory. The grave has no terror for the man or woman who is in Christ Jesus. The Gospel takes that enemy out of the way.

Free from Sin

I also used to think that all my sins would be revealed in front of the Great White Throne. I used to imagine that every sin I had committed in childhood and in secret, every secret thought and every evil desire, would be made public before the assembled universe—that everything done in the dark would be brought to light. But thanks be to God, the Gospel tells me that my sins are all *"put away"* (Heb. 9:26) in Christ! Because of His great love for me, God has taken all my sins and cast them behind His back. That is a safe place to have sin, for God never turns back. He always marches on. He will never see your sins if they are behind His back. That is one of His own illustrations. *"Thou hast in love to my soul delivered it from the pit of corruption: for thou hast cast all my sins behind thy back"* (Isa. 38:17).

This does not just apply to some of my sins. He has taken them *all* out of the way. There is no condemnation for those who are in Christ Jesus (Rom. 8:1). You may pile up your sins until they rise up like a dark mountain and then multiply them by ten thousand for those you cannot think of, and after you have tried to enumerate all the sins you have ever committed, just let me bring in one verse and that mountain will melt away: *"The blood of Jesus Christ his Son cleanseth us from all sin"* (1 John 1:7).

In Ireland, a teacher once asked a little boy if there was anything that God could not do. The little fellow said, "Yes, He cannot see my sins through the blood of Christ." That is just what He cannot do! The blood covers them.

Is it not good news to get rid of your sin? You are a sinner, but if you believe the Gospel, your sins will be taken away. *"Believe on the Lord Jesus Christ, and thou shalt be saved"* (Acts 16:31). You will be freed from all your sins. As I wrote earlier, that is something that the Law of Moses could not do for you. By believing, or by receiving the Gospel, Christ becomes yours. Just think, you are invited to accept the Gospel. You are invited to make an exchange: to get rid of all your sins and to take Christ in place of them. Is that not wonderful? What a foolish person you will be if you do not make the bargain! The Lord says, "I will take your sins and give you Myself in place of them." But a great many people refuse this offer and hold sin to their hearts. May God help you to come to Him right now and receive the Lord Jesus Christ as your Way, your Truth, and your Life.

Free from Judgment

Judgment is another enemy that used to haunt me a great deal. I used to think that it would be a terrible Day when I would be summoned before God. I did not think I could tell until then whether I would be placed at His left hand or at His right. I thought that not until I stood before the Great White Throne of judgment could I tell whether I would hear the voice of God saying, *"Depart from me, ye cursed"* (Matt. 25:41) or *"Enter thou into the joy of thy lord"* (v. 21).

But the Gospel tells me that the question is already settled. Romans 8:1 says, *"There is therefore now no condemnation to them which are in Christ Jesus."* I also want you to read John 5:24, which begins with, *"Verily, verily."* When you see those words, *"Verily, verily,"* in Scripture, you may know there is something very important coming; they mean, "Note what I tell you" or "Truly, truly":

> *Verily, verily, I say unto you, He that heareth my word, and believeth on him that sent me, hath everlasting life, and shall not come into condemnation; but is passed from death unto life.*

The Scripture says that we will not come into condemnation, which means judgment. Well, then, I will not come into judgment for sin! The question has been settled. Christ was judged for me and died in my place, and I go free. Is that not good news?

I heard of a man who prayed that he might lay hold of eternal life. I could not have said "amen" to that prayer. He was looking at it the wrong way. I laid hold of eternal life years ago when I was converted. That man needed to do the same thing. He just needed to receive eternal life as the gift of God. And that is what God wants to give to you today. It is the greatest gift that can be bestowed on anyone down here in this dark world. If an angel came straight from the throne of God and proclaimed to you that God had sent him to offer you anything you might ask for, and that you would have your petition granted, what would you request? There would be only one real cry from your heart, and it would make heaven resound: "Eternal life! Eternal life!" Everything else would vanish into insignificance.

There is nothing a person values more than his life. Suppose that a man who is worth a million dollars is on a wrecked vessel. If he could save his life for just six months by giving that million, he would give it in an instant.

The gift of God is eternal life. Yet, isn't it remarkable that we have to stand and plead and beg men to take this gift? May God help you to take it now! Do not listen to Satan any longer. Reach out the hand of faith and take it now. Believe on the Lord Jesus Christ, and you will be saved. Trust Him to save you now, and there will be no condemnation for you at the Last Day. Death will have lost its sting, the grave and its victory will be safely out of the way, and the judgment will be past for you. Believe the Gospel. Lay hold of eternal life while God is offering it to you. Be reconciled today! Take your stand close to the Cross and you will be saved for time and eternity.

I am told that in Rome, if you go up a few steps on your hands and knees, you are spared nine years of purgatory. But let me tell you that if you take one step right now you are out of "purgatory" for time and eternity. In the doctrine of purgatory, you have two steps into glory: out of self into Christ and then out of purgatory into glory. But there is a true way, in which you take only one step—out of self into glory through Christ—and you are saved. May God help you to take that step now! Flee today to Calvary, my friend, and get under the shadow of the Cross.

In the western United States, in the autumn, when there has not been any rain for months, sometimes the prairie grass catches fire. If a strong wind comes up, the flames shoot up twenty feet high and just roll along at the rate of thirty or forty miles an hour, consuming man and beast. Sometimes hunters find themselves caught out in the middle of this, and when they see the fire coming, what do they do? They know they cannot run as fast as the fire. The fastest horse could not escape from that fire. No, they just take a match and light the grass near them and let the flames sweep on. Then they get into the burnt area and stand there safely. They hear the flames roar as they come along, they see death coming toward them, but they do not fear, they do not tremble, because the fire has swept over the place where they are and there is no danger. There is nothing left for the fire to burn.

There is one mountain peak that the wrath of God has already swept over—"Mount Calvary." The fire has spent its fury on the Son of God. Take your stand there by the Cross, and you will be safe for time and eternity. Escape for your life! Flee to that mountain, and you will be saved this very minute. Oh, may God bring you to Calvary. May you hide under the shadow of the Cross today! Then, let death and the grave come. We will shout, *"Glory to God in the highest"* (Luke

2:14). We will laugh at death and glory in the grave, knowing that we are safe, sheltered by the precious blood of the Lamb. There is no condemnation if we are in Christ Jesus.

BE RECONCILED TODAY

Now is one of the Bible's words that the Devil is afraid of. He knows the influence of that word, so he says, "Do not be in a hurry. There is plenty of time. Do not be saved now." *Tomorrow* is the Devil's word. But the Lord's word is *now* and He says,

> *Come now, and let us reason together, saith the LORD: though your sins be as scarlet, they shall be as white as snow; though they be red like crimson, they shall be as wool.* (Isa. 1:18)

Scarlet and crimson are two colors that you cannot wash out of a fabric. You cannot get the color out without destroying the garment. God says, "Even though your sins are as scarlet and crimson, I will make them as wool and snow. I will do it." That is the way God reasons. The first thing He does is to place the pardon before the sinner. That is a strange way of reasoning, but God's thoughts are not our thoughts. And so, my friend, if you want to be saved, the Lord says He will pardon you.

A few years ago, when Pennsylvania had a Christian governor, there was a young man who was arrested for murder. He was brought before the court, tried, found guilty, and sentenced to death. His friends thought that there would be no trouble getting a reprieve or a pardon. Because the governor was a Christian, they thought that he would not sign the death warrant. But he signed it.

They went to the governor and begged him to pardon the young man, but he said, "No, the law must take its course. The man must die." I think that the mother of the young man also went to the governor and pleaded with him, but he stood firm and said, "No, the man must die."

A few days before the man was to be executed, the governor took the train to the county where the man was imprisoned. He went to the sheriff of the county and said to him, "I want you to take me to that man's cell and leave me alone with him for a little while. Do not tell him who I am until I am gone."

The governor went to the prison and talked to the young man about his soul. He told him that although man had condemned him to be executed, God would have mercy on

73

him and save him if he would accept pardon from Him. He preached Christ and told him how Christ came to seek and to save sinners. Finally, having explained the plan of salvation the best he knew how, he got down and prayed, and after praying, he shook hands with him and said goodbye.

A little while later, the sheriff passed by the condemned man's cell. He called the sheriff to the door of the cell and asked, "Who was that man who talked and prayed with me so kindly?"

The sheriff said, "That was Governor Pollock."

The man turned deathly pale. He threw both of his hands up in the air and said, "Was that Governor Pollock? Was that kindhearted man the governor? Oh, Sheriff, why didn't you tell me? If I had known that was the governor, I would have fallen at his feet and asked for pardon. I would have pleaded for pardon and for my life. Oh, the governor has been here, and I did not know it."

I have good news to tell you. There is One greater than the governor, and He wants to pardon everyone. He does not want you to be condemned. He wants to bring you out from under condemnation. He wants to pardon every soul. Will you accept the pardon or will you despise the gift of God? Will you despise the mercy of God? Oh, right now, while God is imploring you to be reconciled, let me join with your praying mother, your praying father, your godly minister, your Sunday school teacher, and all your praying friends. Let me join my voice with theirs to plead with you to be reconciled today! Make up your mind now, while you are reading these words, that you will not close this book until you are reconciled, and there will be joy in heaven over your decision. Oh, may God bring you to a decision today!

ACCEPT CHRIST'S INVITATION

Some time ago, an Englishman told me a story that illustrates the truth of reconciliation. God is already reconciled. You must just accept what He has done.

The story is this: There was an Englishman who had an only son. As you know, only sons are often pampered, humored, and ruined. This boy became very headstrong, and he and his father often had problems. One day they had a quarrel, and the father and son were very angry at one another. The father said he wished that the boy would leave home and never come back. The boy replied that he would go and would not come into his father's house again until he sent for him. The father said he would never send for him.

Well, the boy went away. But even though a father may give up on a boy, a mother does not. You mothers will understand that, but the fathers may not. You know that there is no love on earth as strong as a mother's love. A great many things may separate a man and his wife, and a great many things may separate a father from a son, but there is nothing in the whole world that can ever separate a true mother from her child. To be sure, there are some mothers who have drunk so much liquor that they have drunk up all their affection. But I am talking about a true mother, and she would not cast off her boy.

This mother began to write to her son and to plead with him to write to his father first, so that his father would forgive him. But the boy answered, "I will never go home until Father asks me to."

She pleaded with the father, but the father said, "No, I will never ask him."

Finally, the mother was so brokenhearted that she fell ill. When she was given up to die by the physicians, her husband, anxious to gratify her last wish, wanted to know if there was anything he could do for her before she died. The mother gave him a look. He knew very well what it meant. Then she said, "Yes, there is one thing you can do. You can send for my boy. That is the only wish on earth that you can gratify. If you do not pity him and love him when I am dead and gone, who will?"

"Well," said the father, "I will send word to him that you want to see him."

"No," she said, "you know he will not come for me. If I am ever going to see him, you must send for him."

At last, the father wrote a letter in his own name, asking the boy to come home. As soon as he got the invitation from his father, he started off to see his dying mother. When he arrived at home, he found his mother dying and his father by her side. The father saw the boy come in, but instead of going to meet him, he went to another part of the room and refused to speak to him. The mother seized her son's hand—how she had longed to hold it tight! She kissed him and then said, "Now, my son, just speak to your father. You speak first, and it all will be over."

But the boy said, "No, Mother, I will not speak to him until he speaks to me."

She took her husband's hand in one hand and the boy's in the other, and spent her dying moments and strength trying to bring about a reconciliation. Right as she was expiring, she could not speak, so she put the hand of the wayward boy into the hand of his father, and passed away. The boy looked at his mother, the father at his wife. At last, the father's heart broke. He opened his arms and took that boy to his heart, and by that mother's body they were reconciled.

Now, that is only a faint example, a poor illustration, because God is not angry with you. Imagine that you are at Calvary's cross. Look at the wounds in the hands and feet of Jesus and at the wound in His side. Gaze on His five wounds! I ask you: Will you not be reconciled? Jesus left heaven and came down to earth so that He might get hold of the vilest sinner and place his hand into the Father's hand. He died so that you and I might be reconciled. If you take my advice, you will not close this book until you are reconciled.

Oh, this Gospel of reconciliation! You are invited to come home now. Your Father wants you to come. Say, like the Prodigal Son, "I will go to my Father," and there will be joy in heaven!

Chapter 4

The Death of Christ

*Surely he hath borne our griefs, and carried
our sorrows: yet we did esteem him stricken,
smitten of God, and afflicted. But he was
wounded for our transgressions, he was
bruised for our iniquities: the chastisement of
our peace was upon him; and with his stripes
we are healed.*
—Isaiah 53:4–5

The little word *our* is used five times in
the above passage of Scripture: our
griefs, our sorrows, our transgressions,
our iniquities, and the chastisement of our
peace. What a Substitute we have in Christ! He
took all our sins, sorrows, and punishment
upon Himself. And yet, we often pick up the
Bible and read the account of His crucifixion
and death, how He suffered in agony, and then

lay the Bible down, go away, and think nothing more about it. However, if we can grasp what Christ accomplished for us on the cross, we can begin to understand all that He offers us in salvation. Therefore, if I can, I want to make the fifty-third chapter of Isaiah real to you. I want to present you with this vital truth: Christ has suffered for each one of us.

When the war was going on, I would read about a great battle that had been fought, in which probably thousands of men had been killed or wounded. However, after reading the article, I would set the paper aside and forget all about it. Finally, I went into the army myself. I saw the dying men. I heard the groans of the wounded. I helped to comfort the dying and bury the dead. I saw the battlefield in all its terrible realities. After I had experienced this, I could not read an account of a battle without it making a profound impression on me.

I wish I could bring before you in living color the sufferings and death of Christ. If I could, I do not believe there would be a dry eye reading this book. I want to speak of His physical suffering, for I think we can grasp that. No one knows or can know what Christ's mental sufferings were.

When a great man has died, we are all eager to hear what his last words were. And if a friend of ours dies, how we treasure his last words, how we repeat them to those who knew him! And we never get tired of talking to our loved ones about how he made his departure from the world. Let us visit Calvary in much the same way. Let us view the last words and actions of Christ before He died on the cross. I will draw from all four Gospels in the account that follows.

GO BACK TO CHRIST'S CRUCIFIXION

Let us go back in our imaginations and suppose that we are living in the city of Jerusalem during the time of Christ. We are walking on one of the streets of Jerusalem on the last day that Jesus spent with His disciples before He was crucified. As we walk, we see a small group of men surrounded by a crowd. Many people are running to see what the excitement is. As we get nearer, we find that it is Jesus with His disciples. We walk down the street with them and watch them enter an ordinary-looking house. We enter also, and there we find Jesus sitting with the disciples. We can see sorrow depicted on His face. His disciples see His grief, but they do not know what has caused it.

Someone has said:

Our Lord's last hours must have been a great mystery to the twelve disciples. He had filled Jerusalem with wonder at the raising of Lazarus; and here He was talking about death—He who could raise a dead man who had been already in his grave four days! What did it mean?

The thirteenth chapter of John tells us why Jesus was so sorrowful.

[Jesus] *was troubled in spirit, and testi-*
fied, and said, Verily, verily, I say unto
you, that one of you shall betray me.
Then the disciples looked one on an-
other, doubting of whom he spake. Now
there was leaning on Jesus' bosom one
of his disciples, whom Jesus loved. Si-
mon Peter therefore beckoned to him,
that he should ask who it should be of
whom he spake. He then lying on Jesus'
breast saith unto him, Lord, who is it?
Jesus answered, He it is, to whom I
shall give a sop, when I have dipped it.
And when he had dipped the sop, he
gave it to Judas Iscariot, the son of Si-
mon.   (vv. 21–26)

The Death of Christ

Soon after, Christ says to Judas, "What you are going to do, do quickly." Then Judas leaves the room. For three years he has seen what the prophets would have been glad to see. For three years he has been associated with the Son of God. For three years Judas has been one of the Twelve. He has sat at the feet of Jesus. He has heard His words of sympathy and love. He has listened to His parables. He has seen Jesus perform His wonderful miracles. He has been exalted to heaven with privileges. Yet, Judas goes out into the night—the darkest night that this world ever saw, the saddest parting that ever took place on this earth—out into darkness, despair, remorse, and death.

Hear him as he goes down those steps, off into the darkness and blackness of the night! He goes to the Sanhedrin and to the chief priests and says to them, "What will you give me if I deliver Him to you?" The Bible tells us that *"they covenanted with him for thirty pieces of silver"* (Matt. 26:15). You can hear the money being counted. Judas puts it into a bag. Then he says, "Give me a band of men, and I will take you where He is."

Thirty pieces of silver was a very small amount. People condemn Judas, but how many are selling Christ for less than he did? Some men and women will sell Him for just a little pleasure. How many are giving up Christ and all hope of heaven for less than thirty pieces of silver!

Though Jesus was deeply sorrowful and anticipating His suffering, it was on that very night that He said to His disciples,

> *Let not your heart be troubled: ye believe in God, believe also in me. In my Father's house are many mansions: if it were not so, I would have told you. I go to prepare a place for you. And if I go and prepare a place for you, I will come again, and receive you unto myself; that where I am, there ye may be also.*
> *(John 14:1–3)*

Instead of the disciples trying to comfort Jesus, He tried to cheer them up.

Now, let us continue the story from the account in Matthew's gospel. He who knew no sin was to bear all our sins. He who was as spotless as the angels of heaven was to suffer for us. From a lonely spot in Gethsemane, His earnest prayers ascend to heaven.

> *Then cometh Jesus with them unto a place called Gethsemane, and saith unto the disciples, Sit ye here, while I go and*

The Death of Christ

pray yonder. And he took with him Peter and the two sons of Zebedee, and began to be sorrowful and very heavy. Then saith he unto them, My soul is exceeding sorrowful, even unto death: tarry ye here, and watch with me. And he went a little farther, and fell on his face, and prayed, saying, O my Father, if it be possible, let this cup pass from me: nevertheless not as I will, but as thou wilt. And he cometh unto the disciples, and findeth them asleep, and saith unto Peter, What, could ye not watch with me one hour? Watch and pray, that ye enter not into temptation: the spirit indeed is willing, but the flesh is weak. He went away again the second time, and prayed, saying, O my Father, if this cup may not pass away from me, except I drink it, thy will be done. And he came and found them asleep again: for their eyes were heavy. And he left them, and went away again, and prayed the third time, saying the same words. Then cometh he to his disciples, and saith unto them, Sleep on now, and take your rest: behold, the hour is at hand, and the Son of man is betrayed into the hands of sinners. Rise, let us be going: behold, he is at hand that doth betray me.   (Matt. 26:36–46)

THE ARREST

Jesus knows that He is about to be betrayed, and He sees the men who are hunting for Him. They are looking around through the olive trees for someone. The Lord knows exactly whom they are searching for, and yet He walks right up to this band of men and asks, "Whom are you looking for?"

And they reply, "We are looking for Jesus of Nazareth."

"I am He."

There is something about that statement that terrifies those men. John's account tells us that when Jesus answers them, they are knocked backward and they fall to the ground. Then Judas comes up and kisses Christ, for he has arranged this as a signal with the Sanhedrin.

When Peter sees what is happening, he draws his sword and cuts off the ear of the servant of the high priest. But Jesus heals the wound at once. He would not let the man suffer. He did not come to destroy life but to save it.

The soldiers seize Jesus. Those hands that had worked so many wonderful miracles, those hands that had often been raised to bless the disciples, are bound. Then Jesus is taken back to Jerusalem. We can see the soldiers and the crowds mocking Him. They lead Him away to Annas first, for he was the father-in-law of Caiaphas, the high priest. And through Annas, He is sent to Caiaphas.

> *The high priest then asked Jesus of his disciples, and of his doctrine. Jesus answered him, I spake openly to the world; I ever taught in the synagogue, and in the temple, whither the Jews always resort; and in secret have I said nothing. Why askest thou me? ask them which heard me, what I have said unto them: behold, they know what I said. And when he had thus spoken, one of the officers which stood by struck Jesus with the palm of his hand, saying, Answerest thou the high priest so? Jesus answered him, If I have spoken evil, bear witness of the evil: but if well, why smitest thou me?* (John 18:19–23)

CHRIST BEFORE THE RULERS

The Sanhedrin is assembled with Caiaphas. Christ is standing before the rulers of the Jews. There are seventy who belong to the Sanhedrin. The law requires that two witnesses must appear against a person on trial before he can be convicted. So they secure false witnesses who come in and testify lies. Then the high priest asks Jesus about the things that the men had testified against Him, but He says nothing. The high priest asks Him, "Are You the Christ, the Son of the Blessed?"

Jesus answers, "I am. And you will see the Son of Man sitting on the right hand of power and coming in the clouds of heaven."

"What need do we have of any further witnesses?" the high priest exclaims. "You have heard the blasphemy. What is your judgment?"

While the trial is going on, Peter is below in the palace, swearing that he never knew Jesus. All of His disciples have forsaken Him. In the morning, Judas would come back and throw down the money he had been paid for betraying innocent blood and would soon be on his way to hang himself.

The verdict of the Sanhedrin comes forth: He is condemned to death. What a sentence! After a short trial, He is pronounced worthy of death! Then they strike Him and spit on Him. In the morning, they take Him to Pilate.

Then led they Jesus from Caiaphas unto the hall of judgment: and it was early; and they themselves went not into the judgment hall, lest they should be defiled; but that they might eat the passover. Pilate then went out unto them, and said, What accusation bring ye against this man? They answered and said unto him, If he were not a malefactor, we would not have delivered him up unto thee. Then said Pilate unto them, Take ye him, and judge him according to your law. The Jews therefore said unto him, It is not lawful for us to put any man to death: that the saying of Jesus might be fulfilled, which he spake, signifying what death he should die. Then Pilate entered into the judgment hall again, and called Jesus, and said unto him, Art thou the King of the Jews? Jesus answered him, Sayest thou this thing of thyself, or did others tell it thee of me? Pilate answered, Am I a Jew? Thine own nation and the chief priests have delivered thee unto me: what hast thou done? Jesus answered, My kingdom is not of this world: if my kingdom were of this world, then would my servants fight, that I should not be delivered to the Jews: but now is my kingdom not from hence. (John 18:28–36)

At this time, the city is filled with strangers from all parts of the country. They have heard that the Galilean prophet has been brought before the Sanhedrin, that He has been condemned, and that all the rulers have to do is to get Pilate's consent and they will put Him out of the way.

Pilate talks with Jesus and then says to the chief priests and to the people, "I find no fault in this Man."

But they shout back, "If you let Him go, you will not be Caesar's friend, for He has stirred up the country from Galilee to here."

"Why," says Pilate, "is He a Galilean?"

And they tell Pilate that He is from Nazareth. When he hears that, he is glad to get rid of the responsibility. "Then I will send Him to Herod," he says.

There were a great many Roman soldiers keeping back the crowds in the streets, the same as our police do on the day of a big event. You can see these soldiers, who have Jesus in custody, going before the crowd, clearing the streets. Herod is glad when Jesus is brought into his presence, for he hopes that He will perform some miracle to gratify his curiosity.

When that doesn't happen, Herod's soldiers despise and mock Jesus, dress Him in a splendid robe, and send Him back to Pilate. You can see the crowd gathered around the judgment hall. They are ready to put Him to death. Someone has said:

All classes of persons conspired to crucify Him. *"The kings of the earth stood*

up, and the rulers were gathered together against the Lord, and against his
Christ" (Acts 4:26): the dissolute, blood-
thirsty Herod; the crafty, worldly
minded Pilate; the idolatrous Gentiles;
and the religious people of Israel—all
united to condemn to death God's holy
Child Jesus.

JESUS OR BARABBAS?

A new thought strikes Pilate. He remembers that it is a custom among the Jews that
on a certain day one prisoner is to be released
to them and go unpunished. So he says to the
Jews, "Which of these two prisoners should I
release, Jesus or Barabbas?"

When Christ's enemies find out what is
going on, they go through the crowd and persuade the people to ask for Barabbas's release.
Pilate asks again, "Which do you want me to
release to you, Jesus or Barabbas?" (Pilate was
asking them to choose between Jesus, who
raised the dead, and Barabbas, who took the
lives of men, whose hands were dripping with
the blood of his fellowmen!) No sooner is the
question put to the crowd than they start
shouting, "Barabbas! Barabbas!"

Pilate asks, "What should I do with Jesus?"

The shout reverberates through the
streets, "Let Him be crucified!" Only a few

days before, the crowd was shouting, "Hosanna to the son of David!"

When Pilate hears this, he turns and washes his hands, saying, "I am innocent of the blood of this just person."

Now, let us imagine the scene when Jesus is taken by the Roman soldiers to be scourged. I never knew until recently what the Roman custom of scourging was. When I first read about it, I could not help weeping and asking Christ to forgive me for not having loved Him more. Sometimes scourging took fifteen minutes, and the man died while undergoing it.

The orders were to put forty stripes, or lashes, one after another, upon Jesus' bare back. See Him stooping as the sins of the world are laid on Him and the whips come down on His bare back, cutting clear through the skin and flesh to the bone.

But he was wounded for our transgressions, he was bruised for our iniquities: the chastisement of our peace was upon him; and with his stripes we are healed.
                                                    (Isa. 53:5)

After they scourge Him, instead of pouring oil into the wounds of Him who came to bind up the brokenhearted and to pour oil into their wounds, they dress Him up again. Some cruel wretch holds out to Him a crown of thorns, which they place on His forehead. The Queen of England wears a crown of gold that is filled with diamonds and precious stones. It is worth millions. But when they came to crown the Prince of Heaven, they gave Him a crown of thorns and placed it on His forehead. And in His hand they put a reed for a scepter.

> *And the soldiers led him away into the hall, called Praetorium; and they call together the whole band. And they clothed him with purple, and platted a crown of thorns, and put it about his head, and began to salute him, Hail, King of the Jews! And they smote him on the head with a reed, and did spit upon him, and bowing their knees worshipped him. And when they had mocked him, they took off the purple from him, and put his own clothes on him, and led him out to crucify him. And they compel one Simon a Cyrenian, who passed by, coming out of the country, the father of Alexander and Rufus, to bear his cross.* (Mark 15:16–21)

ON THE WAY TO CALVARY

Now, imagine that at one of the gates of the city you see a great crowd bursting through.

Two thieves are being brought for execution. Between the two thieves is the Son of God. He carries a cross. Ladies wear small crosses, made of gold and wood and stone, around their necks. However, the cross that the Son of God carried was made out of a heavy tree.

I can see Him reeling and staggering under the weight of the cross. Undoubtedly, He has lost so much blood that He is too faint to carry it; and before they get to the place, it nearly crushes Him to the ground. Meanwhile, the crowd is shouting, "Away with Him! Away with Him!" They consider Him a wicked person.

The crucifixion procession arrives at Calvary a little before nine o'clock in the morning. Then the soldiers take the Son of God and lay Him out on the cross. I can see them binding His wrists to the arms of the cross. After they have Him bound, a soldier comes up with a hammer and nails. He puts one nail into the palm of Jesus' hand. Down comes the hammer without mercy, driving the nail through the bone and flesh and into the wood. The soldier does the same to the other hand. Next, the soldiers bring a long nail and drive it through His feet. Then they gather around the cross and lift it up, and the whole weight of the Son of God comes onto those nails in His hands and feet.

The Death of Christ

ON THE CROSS

Note carefully that Christ has not spoken since He gave words of comfort to the women who mourned Him and followed Him to Calvary. (See Luke 23:27–31.) But at last there is a cry from the cross. What is it? Is it a cry to God to take Him down from the cross? Is it a cry of vengeance? Is He calling down fire on them? No. He cries out, "Father, forgive them, for they do not know what they are doing!" Was there ever such love as that? While they were crucifying Him, He was lifting His heart to God in prayer. His heart seemed to be breaking for those sinners. How He wanted to take them in His arms. How He wanted to forgive them!

There He hangs. Picture those soldiers casting lots for His garments as they crowd around the foot of the cross. The people mock and deride Him and ridicule Him in all sorts of ways. His only response has been, "Father, forgive them, for they do not know what they are doing!" But now He cries out, "My God, my God, why have You forsaken me?"

We are beginning to understand what He suffered physically, but His mental sufferings were too deep for any mortal man to understand. He was dying in the sinner's place, with the sins of the world upon His head. A righteous God could not look on sin, even when it was borne by the eternal Substitute, and He hid His face from Him. Earth had cast Christ out; man had mocked and rejected Him; His own disciples had forsaken Him and fled. And now that God would not look on Him, it nearly broke our Savior's heart, and in the bitter anguish of His soul, He cries, "My God, my God, why have You forsaken me?"

At last He cries, "I am thirsty!" Instead of giving Him a drink of water, they give Him a drink of gall mixed with vinegar. It was about the only thing that He ever asked of the world, and you see how they treated His request.

You who claim that you see no beauty in Christ that you should desire Him (Isa. 53:2), come with me and look at His wounds! See the crown of thorns that was laid upon His forehead by a mocking world. Look at Him as He hangs there. Look at the people who pass by, deriding Him! Hear the two thieves reviling Him. One of them says, "If you are the Christ, save Yourself and us."

Yet, right in the midst of the darkness and gloom, one of those thieves speaks again. It suddenly occurs to him, as he hangs there, "This must be more than man. This must be the true Messiah!" He cries out, "Lord, remember me when You come into Your kingdom." As I wrote earlier, we are interested in hearing about the last word or act of our friends who have died. Here is the last act of Jesus. He snatches the thief from the jaws of death, saying, "Today you will be with Me in paradise."

Again Jesus speaks. What does He say? "It is finished!" Then He bows His head, commends His spirit to God, and dies. Salvation has been accomplished; atonement has been made. His blood has been shed; His life has been given. Undoubtedly, if we could have, we would have seen legions of devils hovering around the cross. The dark clouds of death and hell had come surging up against the heart of the Son of God, and He had driven them back. The waves had gone over Him, just as you have seen waves come together and surge against the rocks, then recede, and then return. He had conquered death and Satan and the world in those last moments. He had tread the winepress alone.

"It is finished!" Perhaps no one who heard those words knew what they meant. But the angels in heaven knew. I can imagine the bells of heaven ringing out and the angels singing, "The God-man is dead! Full restitution has opened the way back into paradise, and all man has to do is to look and live!"

Do you tell me you see no reason why you should love such a Savior? Have you no desire to receive Him and become His?

BEARING OUR GUILT

The following incident was reported in a Christian newspaper, and it touched my heart very deeply. Not long ago, a prominent physician of Denver, Colorado, was called to attend to a patient in the last stages of what appeared to be tuberculosis, but which, upon examination, proved to be simply a wearing away of life—a deterioration of his mind and body. Although well supplied with money, the patient was apparently without friends or relatives. He neither wrote nor received any letters. He seemed to be a stranger to tenderness and love, which enrich and purify the soul, and he appeared to be drifting out of a world in which, for him, all the flowers of the heart had perished. He was a bleak and desolate old man and was quickly moving out of the sunshine into the winter of the grave. After making a thorough examination of the case, the doctor told him that although he could find no specific disease, he was dying.

"I know it," replied the patient.

"But don't you have any idea what brought you to this plight?" inquired the interested man of science.

"It is strange. You have heard a great deal about cases like mine, more as an exaggeration of the imagination than as an actual occurrence. However, strange as it may appear, I am dying—as you say—of a broken heart."

"You surprise me!"

"Yes, I surprise myself. I did not come to your health-giving climate as others do, in search of a longer lease on life, but to die alone and in peace."

"But don't you have any friends?" asked the doctor.

"None that I can claim. My past is sealed with the shadow of a crime, and over my nameless grave not even a memory must hover. I am already dead to all who ever knew my name!"

"You say you are a criminal?" pursued the doctor.

"No, I am not. But I assumed the stigma to shield someone else."

"And that other person was—?"

"My son."

"What was the nature of the crime?"

The physician's curiosity had gotten the better of his discretion. The shadows of twilight were falling around them. Through the open window streamed the soft brilliance of the dying day. Clouds of amethyst and purple floated lazily on the far-off hill. But in the room where the fevered breath was being drawn quick and short, there was a hushed stillness that seemed in keeping with ghostly shadows.

"It was murder."

"And the blame was put on you?"

"Yes. I assumed it and then escaped—not to evade the vengeance of the law, but to spare my beloved son the shame of a felon's death."

"How long ago was that?"

"Twelve years."

"And you have been a wanderer ever since?"

"Ever since."

The feeble pulse was fluttering; the shattered form was growing more rigid every moment.

"Will you tell me no more?" whispered the physician.

"It is all I have to tell!"

The next instant, the man was dead. He had kept his secret and had sacrificed his life in keeping it.

What would we think of that son if we found out that he did not cherish and treasure as his dearest possession the memory of that loving, self-sacrificing father? Could we imagine such despicable and heartless ingratitude?

Certainly not. However, the sacrifice that father made on behalf of his boy is nothing compared with the life of humiliation, pain, sorrow, and shame voluntarily chosen and endured by our blessed Lord. He endured mental anguish and bloody sweat in the garden, physical sufferings and brutal treatment on the cruel cross, and the unspeakable burden of human sin that was laid on Him. Yet, He gladly took all this on Himself so that He might redeem a lost, rebellious world.

Will we give Him nothing in return? Will we banish such love from our hearts? Or, will He see the travail of His soul and be satisfied (Isa. 53:11) because He lives in the deepest affection of those whom He loved and for whom He suffered and died to save? Oh, the height and the depth of our ingratitude and disgrace if we scorn the love of such a Savior and if we do not exalt Him to His rightful place as King in our hearts and lives! God forbid that one person who has ever heard the story of the Cross should be guilty of these things.

Thank God that He is no longer on the cross or in the tomb. He has risen! And He now sits at the right hand of the Father, where He waits to bless His believing people and, in the end, to receive them into His presence and glory!

Chapter 5

Taking God's Way

Our heavenly Father has provided the way of salvation for us through the suffering, death, and resurrection of His Son, Jesus Christ. Jesus said, *"I am the way, the truth, and the life: no man cometh unto the Father, but by me"* (John 14:6). However, many people want to come to God in their own ways. They want to earn their own salvation. And, because of this, they miss their opportunity.

To illustrate the importance of doing things God's way, I want to tell you about a man who was faced with the crucial decision of doing things God's way or his own way. We read about his story in the fifth chapter of 2 Kings. The consequences of this man's decision affected his whole life.

Naaman was a great man in his own country. He held a high position. He was captain of the army of the king of Syria, and the king delighted in honoring him. He was called a lord; he may have been a prince. Perhaps he was second in command, like Prince Bismarck, who was made imperial chancellor of the German Empire. But, in spite of all that, he was a leper, and that cast a dark shadow over his whole life.

There was no physician in Syria who could help him. None of the prominent doctors in Damascus could do him any good. Neither could any in Jerusalem. There was *"no balm in Gilead"* (Jer. 8:22). If he was to get rid of the leprosy, the power must come from on high. It must come from Someone unknown to Naaman, for he did not know God.

WHAT THE SLAVE GIRL KNEW

But I will tell you what they did have in Syria. They had one of God's children there, and she was a little girl, a simple, captive maidservant. Naaman knew nothing about this little Israelite, although she was one of his household. In my imagination, I can see her one day as she tells Mrs. Naaman, her mistress, that there is a prophet in her country who can cure her master of his leprosy.

"I wish," the little girl says, "that my lord were with the prophet who is in Samaria! For he would cure him of his leprosy."

There's faith for you!

"Why," replies the mistress, "what are you talking about? Have you ever heard of anybody being cured of leprosy?"

"Yes," says the girl, "it is true, I assure you. We have prophets down there who can cure anyone."

Finally, someone tells the king what the little maidservant of Israel has said. Now, Naaman has great favor with the king, for he has recently won a great victory. So the king says, "You had better go down to Samaria and see if there is anything to this. I will give you letters of introduction to the king of Israel."

MONEY WILL NOT BUY SALVATION

Yes, the king gave Naaman letters of introduction to Israel's king. That's just the way man works. The idea was that if anybody could help Naaman, it was the king, and that the king had power both with God and man. Oh, my friend, it is a great deal better to know a person who knows God! A person acquainted with God has more power than any earthly ruler. Gold can't do everything.

Naaman travels down to Samaria with his kingly introduction, and he takes with him a great amount of gold and silver. That is man's way again. He is planning on paying for an eminent doctor, and he takes about half a million dollars, as far as I can determine, to pay for the doctor's bill. There are a great many people who would willingly pay that sum, if with it they could buy the favor of God and get rid of the curse of sin. Yes, if money could do it, how many would buy salvation? But, thank God, salvation is not for sale on the market. You must buy it at God's price, and that is *"without money and without price"* (Isa. 55:1). Naaman found that out.

And now, my dear friend, did you ever ask yourself: Which is worse—the leprosy of sin or the leprosy of the body? I would a thousand times rather have the leprosy of the body eating out my eyes and my feet and my arms, I would rather be loathsome in the sight of my fellowmen, than die with the leprosy of sin in my soul and be damned. Oh, how sin has pulled men down! The leprosy of the body is bad, but the leprosy of sin is a thousand times worse. It has cast angels out of heaven; it has ruined the best and strongest men who ever lived in the world. Oh, how it has pulled men down! The leprosy of the body could not do that.

But, to proceed, there is one thing about Naaman that I like, and that is his earnestness of purpose. He was thoroughly in earnest. He was quite willing to take the advice of this little maid and to travel a long distance. A great many people say, "Oh, I don't like such and such a minister. I want to know where he comes from and what he has done and whether he is ordained."

My dear friend, never mind the minister. It is the message you want. If someone were to send me a telegram and the news were important, I wouldn't stop to ask about the messenger who brought it. I would want to read the news. I would look at the message and not at the person who brought it. Or, if I got lost in the city of London, I would be willing to ask anybody which way to go, even if it were only someone who shines shoes. It is the directions I want, not the person who directs me.

It is the same way with God's message. The Good News is everything; the minister is nothing. The Syrians looked down with contempt on the Israelites. And yet, this great man was willing to listen to the words of this little girl and to receive good news from her. There was only one drawback. Although he was willing to take the advice of the little girl, he was not, at first, willing to accept the remedy.

THE STUMBLING BLOCK OF PRIDE

The remedy that Elisha the prophet offered Naaman was a terrible blow to his pride.

I have no doubt that he expected a magnificent reception from the king of Israel, to whom he brought his letters of introduction. He had been victorious on many fields of battle and he held high rank in the army. Perhaps we may call him Major General Naaman of Syria. As I wrote earlier, he may have been even higher in rank than that. Moreover, since he carried kingly credentials, he expected, no doubt, a distinguished reception. But the king of Israel, instead of rushing out to meet Naaman when he heard of his arrival and purpose, simply tore his clothes and said, "Am I God, to kill and to make alive?"

However, when Elisha heard about this, he sent word to the king, saying, "Why have you torn your clothes? Let him come to me and he will know that there is a prophet in Israel." And I can imagine Naaman, in his pride, reasoning in this way: "Certainly this prophet will feel very important and will be extremely flattered that I, the great Syrian general, would come and call on him."

And so, probably full of those proud thoughts, he drives up to the prophet's humble dwelling with his chariot, four-in-hand, and his splendid entourage. Nobody comes out to greet him, and so he sends in his message: "Tell the prophet that Major General Naaman of Syria has arrived and wishes to see him."

Elisha takes it very coolly. He does not come out to see him but sends his servant to tell him that if he dips seven times in the Jordan River, he will be clean.

Now, that was a terrible blow to his pride! I can imagine him saying to the servant, "What did you say? Did I understand you correctly? Dip seven times in the Jordan? Why, we call the Jordan River a ditch in our country!"

But the only answer he receives is, "The prophet says, 'Go and wash in the Jordan seven times, and your skin will be restored, and you will be clean.'"

I can imagine Naaman's indignation as he asks, "Are not Abana and Pharpar, rivers of Damascus, better than all the waters of Israel? May I not wash in them and be clean?" And he turns and goes away in a rage.

The fact is that the Jordan never has had any great reputation as a river. It flows into the Dead Sea, and that sea has never had a harbor. In Elisha's day, the banks of the Jordan were not half as beautiful as the banks of the rivers of Damascus, for Damascus was one of the most beautiful cities in the world. It is said that when Mohammed saw it, he turned his head aside because he was afraid that it would divert his thoughts from heaven.

"Here I am," Naaman says, "a great conqueror, a successful general on the battlefield, holding the very highest rank in the army, and yet this prophet does not even come out to meet me. He simply sends a message! Why, I thought he would surely come out to me and stand and call on the name of the Lord his God and wave his hand over the place and heal my leprosy."

"I THOUGHT"

There's that phrase! Almost every person I've ever known who was confronted with his sins has said, "Yes, but *I thought* so and so."

"Mr. Moody," people say, "I will tell you what I think. I will tell you my opinion."

Isaiah 55:8 tells us that God's thoughts are not our thoughts and that His ways are not our ways. And so it was with Naaman. In the first place, he thought that a good, large doctor's fee was all that he needed and that it would settle everything. And besides that, he thought that going to the king with his letters of introduction would certainly be sufficient. Yes, those were Naaman's first thoughts.

I thought. Exactly so. He turned away in rage and disappointment. He had thought that the prophet would come out to him very humbly and very subserviently and tell him to do some great things. Instead of that, Elisha, who was probably busy writing, did not even come to the door or the window. He merely sent out the message, "Tell him to dip seven times in the Jordan."

And Naaman went away, saying, "I thought, I thought, I thought." I have heard that story so often that I am tired of it. I will tell you exactly what I think about it and what I would advise you to do: Give it up, and take God's words, God's thoughts, and God's ways. I never yet knew a person who was converted exactly in the time and way he expected to be. I have heard people say, "Well, if I am ever converted, it won't be in a Methodist church. You won't catch me there." Now, I never knew a person who said that who, in the end, was not converted in a Methodist church, if he was converted at all. A person, to be converted, has to give up his will, his ways, and his thoughts. God usually leads him in quite a different direction than he expects.

And so, after Naaman's anger has abated and he has cooled down a little, another way of looking at the situation is presented to him. This proves to be the best way, although his pride has been terribly humbled.

THE SIMPLE REMEDY

While Naaman is debating in his mind about all this and trying to figure out the best thing to do, one of his servants comes up to him and makes a very sensible remark. "My lord," he says, "if the prophet had instructed you to do some great thing, you would have done it, wouldn't you? How much more, then, should you do it when he says to you, 'Wash and be clean.'"

Yes, there is a great deal of truth in that. If Elisha had said to him, "Go back to Syria on your hands and knees," he most likely would have done it. If he had said, "Go back all the way on one foot," he would have tried to do it. Or, if Elisha had said, "Give me ten thousand pieces of gold," no doubt he would have given it. But, simply to tell him to dip in the Jordan River seven times, why, on the surface, it seemed absurd! But Naaman's servant suggests to him that he had better go down to the Jordan and try the remedy, since it is a very simple one.

I can imagine Naaman, still reluctant to believe in it, saying, "Why, if there is such cleansing power in the waters of the Jordan, why doesn't every leper in Israel go down and dip in them and be healed?"

"Well, but, you know," urges the servant, "now that you have come a hundred and fifty miles, don't you think you had better do what he tells you? After all, you can just try it. And he sent word distinctly, my lord, that your skin would be restored."

So Naaman accepts this word in season. His anger is cooling down. He has gotten over the first wave of his indignation, and so he says that he might as well try it. This is the starting point of his faith, although he still thinks it is a foolish thing and cannot bring himself to believe that the result will be what the prophet has said.

How many people have told me right to my face they do not believe that a person can be saved simply by obeying God! Faith, they think, is not enough; they must do something. They want to believe that there must be a little asking and reasoning and striving and wrestling with God before they can get the blessing.

FOOLISH QUESTIONS

I remember praying with a man for his conversion. Just when I thought he had been convicted of his sin, he said, "Mr. Moody, the Bible mentions a mysterious person named Melchizedek. Who do you think he was?"

And then there have been others who have asked me right when I have been praying with them that their sins might be taken away, "Do you believe in infant baptism?"

My friend, you do not need to trouble yourself about these questions. If you want to be saved, just do as the Bible tells you to do.

UNCONDITIONAL SURRENDER

When General Grant was besieging a town that was the stronghold of the Southern Confederacy, some of the Confederate officers sent word that they would leave the city if he would let them go with their men. But General Grant sent word, "No, nothing but an unconditional surrender!" Then they sent word that they would go if he would let them take their flag with them. But the answer was, "No, an unconditional surrender." At last, the beleaguered walls were broken down and the city was entered, and then the enemy made a complete and unconditional surrender. It was the same way with Naaman. His will was conquered, subdued, and broken. He had faith, and he surrendered. He got to the point where he was willing to obey, and the Scripture tells us, *"To obey is better than sacrifice"* (1 Sam. 15:22).

Naaman goes down to the river and takes the first dip. I can imagine him looking at himself as he comes up and saying to his servant, "There—I am no better off than I was when I went in. If one-seventh of the leprosy were gone, I would be content."

Well, he goes down a second time and comes up puffing and blowing, as much a leper as he ever was. He goes down the third, fourth, and fifth time, with the same result. He is still a leper. And the people standing on the banks of the river probably said, as they certainly would today, "That man is out of his mind!"

When he comes up the sixth time, he looks at himself and says, "Ah, no better! What a fool I have made of myself! How they will laugh at me! I wouldn't want the generals and aristocracy of Damascus to know, for all the world, that I have been dipping in the Jordan in this way. However, since I have gone this far, I'll make the seventh plunge."

He has not lost faith altogether. He goes down the seventh time and comes up again. When he looks at himself, he shouts aloud for joy. "Look, I am well! My leprosy is all gone, all gone! My skin has been restored. It is like the skin of a little child! I never heard of such a thing. I never felt so happy in my whole life. I thought I was a great and happy man when I accomplished that victory on the battlefield. But, thank God, now I am the happiest man alive!"

Naaman comes up out of the Jordan, puts on his clothes, and goes back to the prophet. He wants to pay him. It's the same old story.

Naaman wants to give money for his cure. How many people want to do the same thing today! Why, it would have spoiled the story of grace if the prophet had taken anything. You may give a contribution to God's cause, not to purchase salvation, but because you have been saved and are thankful to Him. The prophet Elisha refused to take anything, and I can imagine that no one felt more joyful than he did.

When Naaman starts back to Damascus, he is a very different man from what he had been. The dark cloud has gone from his mind. He is no longer a leper; he is no longer afraid of dying from a loathsome disease. He lost the leprosy in the Jordan when he did what the man of God told him to do. And, if you will obey the voice of God, even as you are reading this, the burden of your sins will fall from you and you will be cleansed. It is all done by the power of faith.

You may be sure that when Naaman arrived home, there was no small stir in his household. I can just see his wife when he gets back. She has been watching and looking out the window for him with a great burden on her heart. And when she asks him, 'Well, my husband, how are you?" I can see the tears running down his cheeks as he says, "Thank God, I am well!" They embrace each other and pour out mutual expressions of rejoicing and happiness. And the servants are just as glad as their master and mistress, because they have been waiting eagerly for the news.

There never was a happier household than Naaman's, after he was free of the leprosy. And, my friend, it will be the same with your own household if you will only get rid of the leprosy of sin today. Not only will there be joy in your own heart and joy in your home, but there will also be joy among the angels of heaven.

In this account of Naaman, another thought is suggested to us that shows what Naaman's faith led him to believe. We find it in 2 Kings 5:15

> *And he returned to the man of God, he and all his company, and came, and stood before him: and he said, Behold, now I know that there is no God in all the earth, but in Israel: now therefore, I pray thee, take a blessing of thy servant.*

I particularly want to call your attention to the words *I know*. He has no hesitation about it. He doesn't qualify his words. Naaman doesn't say, "I think." Instead, he says, "I know there is a God who has the power to forgive sins and to cleanse leprosy."

Then, an additional thought is suggested to us. Naaman left only one thing in Samaria, and that was his sin, his leprosy. The only thing that God wants you to leave with Him is your sin. Yet, it is the only thing that you do not seem to feel that you have to give up.

"Oh," you say, "I love sin. It is so delightful that I can't give it up. I know that God wants it, so that He may make me clean, but I can't give it up."

Why, what absolute insanity it is for you to love leprosy. And yet, that is your condition! I can hear someone saying, "Yes, but I don't believe in sudden conversions."

Don't you? Well, how long did it take Naaman to be cured? The seventh time that he went down, the leprosy went away! Read about the great conversions that are recorded in the Bible, like Saul of Tarsus, Zacchaeus, and many others. How long did it take the Lord to bring them about? They were effected in a minute. We are born and shaped in iniquity, *"dead in trespasses and sins"* (Eph. 2:1). However, when spiritual life comes, it comes in a moment, and we are freed from both sin and death.

WHERE WILL YOU BE IN A HUNDRED YEARS?

One day, as I was walking down the street, I heard some people laughing and talking. One of them said, "Well, it doesn't make any difference. It won't matter a hundred years from now." The thought flashed across my mind, Will it make no difference? Where will you be a hundred years from now?

Young person, just ask yourself the question, Where will I be? Some of you who are getting on in years may be in eternity ten years from now. Where will you be, on the left or on the right hand of God? I can't tell what your thoughts on the subject are, but I can tell you mine.

Everyone reading this book right now will be gone in a hundred years. Some will probably be gone in less than a week or in less than a month or a year. At most, we will all be gone in just a few more years. I ask you once again, Where will you spend eternity? Where will you be a hundred years from now?

THE HAUNTING QUESTION

I heard of a young man who came from Europe a few years ago, bringing letters to distinguished physicians from his king, who had written, "This man is a personal friend of mine and we are afraid that he is going to lose his reason. Do all that you can for him."

One doctor that the young man went to see asked him if he had lost a dear friend in his own country or if he had lost a position of importance. He said that he had not. Then the doctor asked him what was weighing on his mind. The man answered, "My father, my grandfather, and myself were brought up as unbelievers, and for the last two or three years this thought has been haunting me: Where will I spend eternity? The thought of it follows me day and night."

The doctor said, "You have come to the wrong physician, but I will tell you of One who can cure you." And he told him about Christ and read to him the fifty-third chapter of Isaiah, emphasizing verse five: *"With his stripes we are healed."*

The young man said, "Doctor, do you believe that?"

The doctor told him that he did. And he prayed with the young man and helped him wrestle through his doubts. At last, the clear light of Calvary shone on his soul. Later, he was writing to this doctor as only one Christian can to another. He finally had settled the question in his own mind about where he would spend eternity. And I ask you to settle it before you close this book. It is for you to decide. Will you spend eternity with the saints and martyrs and prophets or in the dark caverns of hell, amid blackness and darkness forever? Be in a hurry to be wise, for *"how shall we escape, if we neglect so great salvation"* (Heb. 2:3)?

DECIDE BEFORE IT IS TOO LATE

At my church in Chicago, I was closing the meeting one day, when a young soldier got up and begged the people to decide for Christ at once. He said he had just come from a terrible scene. A friend of his, who had enlisted with him, had a father who was always pleading with him to become a Christian, and in reply he always said that he would do so when the war was over.

Finally, his friend was wounded and was put into the hospital, but he got worse and was gradually sinking. One day, a few hours before he died, a letter came from his sister. Oh, it was such an earnest letter! He was too weak to read, so this soldier read it to him. He did not seem to understand it until he heard the last sentence, which read, "Oh, my dear brother, when you get this letter, won't you accept your sister's Savior?"

The dying man sprang up from his cot and said, "What did you say? What did you say?" Then, falling back on his pillow, he feebly exclaimed, "It is too late! It is too late!"

My dear friend, thank God it is not too late for you today. The Master is still calling you.

Taking God's Way

Let each one of us, young or old, rich or poor, come to Christ at once. He will cleanse us of the leprosy of sin and make us clean and white by His own precious blood!

Chapter 6

"Remember"

But Abraham said, Son, remember that thou in thy lifetime receivedst thy good things, and likewise Lazarus evil things: but now he is comforted, and thou art tormented.
—Luke 16:25

Naaman almost missed his chance to be healed of leprosy. And many people miss their opportunity to receive salvation because they want to do things their own way. Yet, such a course of action has eternal consequences. The Scriptures describe hell as a place where there is *"fire that never shall be quenched"* and *"where their worm dieth not"* (Mark 9:43–44). I believe that the *"worm"* that is spoken of is the memory. I believe that this is what is going to make hell so terrible for those who have lived in a country where the Gospel has often been preached. They will think about what they might have been. They will think about how they might have spent eternity in the world of light.

We read in Luke 16 that a certain rich man has died and is now in another world. His soul has left his body, he has gone beyond time, and he is now in another world. Some say that when people preach about hell, it is only to terrify people, to alarm them. Now, I am no alarmist, and would never terrify anyone in order to scare him into the kingdom of God. But, at the same time, if I am to be a messenger for God, I must tell the whole message. I must not keep back any part of the Word of God. The same Christ who told us of heaven with all its glories, told us of hell with all its horrors. And no one can accuse Christ of revealing this picture of hell just to terrify people or to alarm them. He was speaking of something real.

I have read some descriptions of hell, but I have never read one more terrifying than this one. A rich man was *"clothed in purple and fine linen"* and *"fared sumptuously every day"* (v. 19) while he was in this world, but when we catch a glimpse of him in another world, we find him in hell, crying out in torment.

Some tell us that there is no hell and some tell us that there is no heaven. If I had to give up one, I would have to give up the other. The same Bible that tells us about heaven, tells us about hell. The same Savior who came down from heaven to tell us about heaven, told us about hell. He spoke about escaping the damnation of hell, and there is no one who has lived since Christ who could tell us as much about it as He.

If there is no hell, let us burn our Bibles. Why spend so much time studying the Bible? Why spend so much time and so much money building churches? Let us turn our churches into places of commerce or amusement. Let us eat, drink, and be merry, for we will soon be gone if there is no life after death. Let us build a monument to Paine and Voltaire. Let us build a tomb over Christianity and shout over it, "There is no hell to receive us. There is no God to condemn sin. There is no heaven. There is no afterlife!"

We need to be serious about this question of eternity. If there is a heaven and a hell, then let us act as God wants us to act. God was in earnest when He gave Christ to die for us. Christ was in earnest when He went to Calvary and suffered that terrible death. It was to save us from that terrible hell. If I did not believe there is a hell, you would not find me going from town to town, spending day and night preaching and proclaiming the Gospel and urging men to escape the damnation of hell. I would take things easy.

Oh, my friend, I cannot help believing it! And if you are in doubt about it, why not be honest? If you believe you have a Creator, why not ask Him to give you understanding about the future? There was a time when I did not believe in hell, but God revealed the truth to me. It is a matter of revelation. It is Satan who is telling us that there is no life after death and no hell, because the Word of God teaches these things very plainly.

If there is a hell, we'd better find out before we get there. It would be a great deal better for us to find out here and to take it seriously, than to be laughing and joking about it. It makes me feel very sad to hear people speaking so flippantly about hell and making jokes about it. God is not to be trifled with. Think of the rich man in that lost world, crying for one drop of water and asking Abraham to send someone to comfort him. But no one can, because a chasm has been fixed that no one can cross. God Himself has established that gulf.

The time is coming when there will be a separation. The time is coming when that praying wife and that godless, Christless husband will be separated. The time is coming when that devout mother will be lifted up to heaven and that scorning, unbelieving son will be cast down to hell, unless he is wise and accepts salvation.

MEMORY IN HELL

Now, what I want to emphasize to you is that there is memory in hell. What did Abraham say to the rich man? *"Remember."* Oh, may this portion of Scripture be engraved on your heart!

"Remember." God wants you to wake up and remember before it is too late. It is much better for a person to be wise and to stop and think while he has the privilege of changing his mind, if he is wrong, than it is for him to go on like a madman and be cast into the prison of hell. Then he will have to think. Yes, then memory will be eager to do something about it, but it will be too late to make a change.

Twice I have been at the point of death. One time I was drowning and just as I was going down for the third time, I was rescued. In the twinkling of an eye, my whole life came flashing across my mind. I cannot tell you how it happened. I cannot tell you how a whole life can be crowded into a second of time. Yet, everything that I had done since childhood came flashing across my mind. And, I believe that when God touches the secret springs of our memories, every one of our sins will come back, and if they have not been blotted out by the blood of the Lord Jesus Christ, they will haunt us as eternal ages roll on. We can say that we will forget, but we cannot forget if God says, "Remember!"

People talk about there being a recording angel who keeps the records of our lives. I have an idea that when we get to heaven or into eternity, we will find that the recording angel has been ourselves. God will make each one of us keep his own record. Our memories will keep the records and when God says, *"Remember,"* they will all flash across our minds. It won't be God who will condemn us; it will be ourselves. We will condemn ourselves and we will stand before God speechless.

Imagine a man who has been in prison for five years. If you were to ask that man what makes prison so terrible for him, the walls, the bars, or the hard work, he would tell you that it is none of these things. He would tell you that what makes prison so terrible for him is his memory. And I have an idea that if we went down into the lost world, we would discover that memory is what makes hell so terrible for those who are there—the recollection that they once heard the Gospel, that they once had Christ offered to them, that they once had the privilege of being saved, but that they made light of the Gospel, they neglected salvation, they rejected the offer of mercy. And now, even if they wanted to receive salvation, they could not.

A MISSIONARY SPIRIT IN HELL

We find that this rich man had a specific desire to get out of that place of torment. He had a missionary spirit when he got there, for he said, "Send someone to my father's house to warn my five brothers. Oh, send someone to tell them not to come to this place of torment!"

It would have been better if he had had a missionary spirit before he got there! And it would be better for you to wake up and come to the Lord Jesus Christ and go to work to save your friends while you still have the ability to pray, while you are still in this world. Your missionary spirit won't help you when you are in hell; it won't help you when you are in the lost world. Yes, memory, memory!

PAINFUL MEMORIES

If Cain is in that lost world, no doubt he can remember the pleading of his brother, Abel. He

can remember how he looked when he killed
him. He can hear that piercing cry today. He
has not forgotten it. All these long years, Cain
has remembered what he might have been, how
he despised the God of grace, and how he lost
his soul. Thousands of years have rolled away,
but Cain still has to think. He cannot help
thinking.

I have no doubt that Judas remembers
how Christ preached the Sermon on the Mount
and how Christ looked when He wept over Jerusalem. He can see those tears today. He can
hear Christ's voice, crying out over Jerusalem,

> *Jerusalem, Jerusalem, thou that killest*
> *the prophets, and stonest them which are*
> *sent unto thee, how often would I have*
> *gathered thy children together, even as a*
> *hen gathereth her chickens under her*
> *wings, and ye would not!   (Matt. 23:37)*

He hears that cry. He can see that kind,
mild, gentle look of the Son of God. He can
hear Christ saying to him in Gethsemane,
"Betrayest thou the Son of man with a kiss?"
(Luke 22:48). Yes, memory is at work. His
memory had awakened even before he died,
when he went out and destroyed himself, taking his remorse and despair with him into the
lost world.

PAY ATTENTION TO THE WARNING

Do you think that those pre-flood people have forgotten how Noah pleaded with them? They laughed at the ark. I have no doubt that if you had gone and preached to them a week before the flood and told them that there is a hell, not one of them would have believed it. If you had told them that there was going to be a deluge and that God was going to sweep them away from the earth, they would not have believed it. But their unbelief did not change the fact that they perished. Didn't the flood come and take them all away?

If you had gone to Sodom and told the Sodomites that God was going to destroy their city, they would have laughed at you, just as people laugh at and make light of hell. But the unbelief of the Sodomites did not change the fact of their destruction. Didn't God destroy the cities in the plain of the Jordan River?

It was the same way with Jerusalem. Christ described how destruction would come upon the city, and people mocked Him and crucified Him. But look down the flow of time! In forty short years, Titus came up against that city and besieged it, and a million people perished within its walls. Yes, those Jerusalem sinners in the lost world today can remember how Christ wept over Jerusalem, how He walked their streets, how He went into the temple and preached, and how He pleaded with them to escape for their lives and to flee the damnation of hell. But they had mocked Him; they had laughed at Him; they had made light of these things until it was too late; and they are gone now.

Oh, may God wake you up and may every man and woman reading this book escape for their lives before it is too late! *"How shall we escape,"* said the apostle, *"if we neglect so great salvation?"* (Heb. 2:3).

NO BIBLE IN THE LOST WORLD

There will be no Bible in the lost world to be a lamp to your feet and a light to your path, to guide you to eternal mansions. You make light of the Bible now, you laugh at its teachings, but bear in mind, there will be no Bible in the lost world. You have a Bible here. Hadn't you better read it? Hadn't you better believe it?

I have no doubt that if you had gone to that rich man of our Scripture text a week before he was taken away, he would have told you that he did not believe in the Bible, that he did not believe in a place of torment, that he did not believe a word of it. But did that change the truth? He found out when it was too late. And there was no Bible there to help him out. There was no minister there to go and preach to him. Yes, bear in mind that, if you get into that lost world, there will be no minister to pray for you. No earnest sermons will be preached there. It will be too late then.

And there will be no Sunday school teacher there. I am directing this to some young people who attend Sunday school and who have praying teachers. Bear in mind, you will have no teacher there to weep over you, to pray for you, to plead with you to come to Christ.

I may be speaking to some young man whose friend has come and put his hand on his shoulder and asked him to come to Christ. You made light of that, young man. You laughed at him and argued with him. Bear in mind, no friend will come and put his hand on your shoulder and speak loving words to you there. *"Remember."* If you have friends who are very concerned about your soul's salvation and are pleading for you in prayer, treat them kindly. You will not have them in that lost world. Do not laugh at them. It is God who has sent the loving message to you.

I may be speaking to some young man who has a godly, praying mother. You are on a collision course with destruction and are breaking your mother's heart. Fill her heart with joy today by telling her that you have accepted her God as your God, her Savior as your Savior, that you are not going down to death and destruction, but that you will meet her in glory. Oh, may God meet every person who is reading this book, and may every eye and heart be opened to receive the truth!

There is a song that my associate, Mr. Ira Sankey, sings, called "Jesus of Nazareth Passeth By." But, bear in mind, you will not hear that song in the lost world. Or, if you do, it will not be true. He does not pass that way. He is passing your way today! I beg of you, do not make light of the Lord Jesus and His offer of mercy. He comes to save you from a terrible hell. He wants to redeem your soul today.

Right now, you have a golden opportunity. Jesus is truly passing your way. Do not doubt that He has been near you as you have been reading. In the course of my meetings, a great many people have come into the inquiry room and said to me, "I have accepted Christ. I have found Him tonight." The Lord Jesus Christ is truly in our midst. He is saving some. Why shouldn't He save you also?

While He is passing by and so many are believing in Him, why won't you receive Him? My friend, God does not want you to perish. He wants you to be saved. God does not want one soul to be lost. He wants everyone to be in glory. And if you will accept His Son as a gift from Him, if you will accept the Lord Jesus, you can be saved.

AN UNBELIEVING MOTHER

I was standing by the door to the inquiry room a few months ago when I saw a lady weeping. I spoke to her, but a woman grabbed her by the hand and pushed her away from me. "What is the trouble?" I asked.

"This is my daughter," she said, "and I don't want her to be associated with Christians. I hate Christians."

I tried to reason with that mother but she pulled her weeping daughter away even though her daughter was pleading with her to stay.

Are you such a mother? May God have mercy on you! It would be a thousand times better for your children to be associated with Christians than it would be to have them go down to death and be associated with fiends for eternity. All workers of iniquity will be cast into the lake of fire, but those whose names are written in the Book of Life will have a right to the Tree of Life and will walk the crystal pavement of heaven. Oh, may God help you to be wise today, to flee from your old friends and associates, and to lay hold of eternal life! Do not trifle with this great subject. Be wise, and accept salvation from God in the way in which He has provided.

AN UNFEELING SON

I was once told about a father whose son had broken his mother's heart. After the mother's death, the son had gone from bad to worse. One night, he was going out to spend the night in depravity, and the old man went to the door and said, "My son, I want to ask a favor of you tonight. You have not spent one evening with me since your mother was buried, and I have been so lonesome without her and without you. And now I want you to spend the evening with me. I want to have a talk with you about the future."

The young man said, "No, Father, I don't want to stay. It is too depressing here at home."

"Won't you stay for my sake?"

The son said that he would not. At last, the old man said, "If I cannot persuade you to stay, if you are determined to go down to destruction and to break my heart as you have broken your mother's—for these gray hairs cannot stand it much longer—you will not go until I make one more effort to save you."

The Father threw open the door. Then he lay down on the threshold and said, "If you go out tonight, you must go over this old body of mine."

What did that young man do? He leaped over his father and went on to his ruin.

Now, I do not think that there is a man or woman who would deny that that young man was an ungrateful wretch. Yet, did you ever stop and think that God has given you His Son? Yes, He has laid Him, as it were, right across your path, so that you might not go down to hell. And if you do go to hell, it will be over the murdered body of God's Son. You will have to trample the blood of Christ under your feet.

GOD'S WAY OF ESCAPE

God is always ready to forgive us. No sooner did the news reach heaven that Adam had fallen, than God came down and made a way of escape. God loved the world so much that He gave Christ to die for us, so that you and I might live. Do not make light of the blessed Savior. Do not keep that scornful look on your face but lift up your heart to God and say, *"God be merciful to me a sinner"* (Luke 18:13). Receive the gift of God!

If the Spirit of God is striving with you, let me plead with you to treat Him kindly. Bear in mind that God has said, *"My spirit shall not always strive with man"* (Gen. 6:3). I believe that you have been awakened and that the Spirit of God has been striving with you. And now, let me plead with you as a friend. Just give yourself up to the leading of the Spirit of God. The Spirit of God will lead you in the right way. He never makes any mistakes. God has sent Him from heaven into this world to lead us out of darkness into light, and the Spirit is drawing you to Christ. Do not resist Him; do not reject Him. I do not ask you to believe what I say. All I ask is that you believe what God tells you, that you believe what the Spirit of God will reveal to you about Christ. If the Spirit of God is striving with you, do not quench Him or resist Him. Just open the door of your heart and let Him come in. It will be a thousand times better for you in this life and in the life to come.

RESPOND IMMEDIATELY

A few years ago, I was about to close a meeting, and I said, "Are there any here who would like to have me remember them in prayer? I would like them to stand up!"

A man stood up, and when I saw him, my heart leaped for joy. I had been concerned about him for a long time. I went to him as soon as the meeting was over, took him by the hand, and said, "You are taking a stand for God, aren't you?"

"I want to," he said, "and I have made up my mind to be a Christian, but there is one thing that stands in my way."

"What is that?" I asked.

"Well," he said, "I lack moral courage. If (naming a friend of his) had been here tonight, I would not have stood up. And I am afraid that when he hears I have risen for prayer, he will begin to laugh at me, and I won't have the moral courage to stand up for Christ."

I said, "If Christ is what He is represented to be in the Bible, He is worth standing up for. And if heaven is what we are told it is in the Bible, it is worth living for." He answered that he lacked moral courage, and he was trembling from head to foot. I thought that he was standing on the very threshold of heaven and that one more step would take him in. I thought that he would take the step that night. As I talked and prayed with him, the Spirit seemed to be striving greatly with him, but he did not surrender to God. Night after night, he came, and the Spirit still strove with him.

However, that same thing held him back. He lacked moral courage. At last, the Spirit of God, who had striven with him so mightily, seemed to leave him, and there was no more striving. He stopped coming to church, was off among his old friends, and would not greet me on the street. He was too ashamed to do so.

About six months later, I got a message from him, asking me to come see him. I found him on what he thought was his deathbed. He wanted to know if there was any hope for him at the eleventh hour. I tried to tell him that there is hope for any man who will accept Christ. I prayed with him and visited him day after day.

Contrary to all expectations, he began to recover. When he was convalescent, I visited him one day when he was sitting in front of his house. I sat by his side and said, "You will soon be well enough to come to church. When you are, you are going to come and confess Christ boldly, aren't you?"

"Well," he said, "when I thought I was dying, I promised God that I would serve Him, and I made up my mind to be a Christian, but I am not going to be one right now. Next spring I am going to go over near Lake Michigan, buy a farm, and settle down. And then I am going to become a Christian."

"How dare you talk in that way!" I said. "How do you know that you are going to live until next spring?"

"I've never felt better in my life," he said. "I am a little weak but I will soon have my strength back. I have a fresh lease on life and will be well for a good many years yet."

"It seems to me that you are tempting God," I said. And I pleaded with him to take a bold stand for Christ.

"No," he said, "the fact is, I do not have the courage to face my old friends, and I cannot serve God in Chicago."

"If God does not have enough grace to sustain you in Chicago," I said, "He does not have enough grace to sustain you in Michigan."

I urged him to surrender soul and body to the Lord Jesus. But the more I urged him, the more irritated he got, until at last he said, "Well, you do not need to concern yourself anymore about my soul. I will attend to that. If I am lost, it will be my own fault. I will take the risk."

A DREADFUL DEATHBED

I left him, and within a week I got a message from his wife. I went to the house and when his wife met me at the door, she was crying. I said, 'What is the trouble?"

"I have just had a consultation with several physicians. They have all given up my husband to die. They say he cannot possibly live."

"Does he want to see me?" I asked.

"No."

"Then, why did you send for me?"

"I cannot bear to see him die in this terrible state of mind."

"What is his state of mind?"

"He says that his damnation is sealed and that he will be in hell in a little while."

I went into the room but he turned his head away. "How are you?" I asked.

Not a word! He was as silent as death. I spoke a second time but he made no response. I looked him in the face and called him by name and said, "Will you not tell me how you are?"

He turned and stared at me with that awful, deathly look. Then he said, "My heart is as hard as iron. It is too late! My damnation is sealed, and I will be in hell in a little while."

"Don't talk that way," I said. "You can be saved now if you are willing."

"Don't you mock me," he replied. "I know better."

I talked with him and quoted promise after promise, but he said that none of them were for him.

"Christ has come knocking at the door of my heart many times. The last time He came, I promised to let Him in, but when I got well, I turned away from Him again. And now I have to perish without Him."

I continued to talk with him but when I saw that I was doing no good, I threw myself on my knees.

"You can pray for my wife and my children," he said "You do not need to pray for me. It is a waste of time. It is too late!"

I tried to pray, but it seemed as if what he said was true, as if the heavens were as brass over me.

I rose and took his hand. It seemed to me that I was saying farewell to a friend whom I was never to see again in time or in eternity.

He lingered until the sun went down. His wife told me that his last hours were terrible. All he said were these dreadful words from Jeremiah 8:20: "The harvest is past, the summer is ended, and I am not saved!" There he lay, and every once in a while he would repeat the awful words, "The harvest is past, the summer is ended, and I am not saved!"

Just as the sun was sinking behind those western prairies, he was going into the arms of death. As he was expiring, his wife noticed that his lips were quivering. He was trying to say something. She leaned over to listen and all she could hear was, "The harvest is past, the summer is ended, and I am not saved!" And then he died and the angels carried him to Judgment.

He lived a Christless life and he died a Christless death. We dressed him in Christless burial clothes and placed him in a Christless coffin. Then we carried him to a Christless grave.

How dismal! How sad!

MAY WE MEET IN GLORY

The harvest may be passing for you. The summer may be ending. Oh, be wise today and accept the Lord Jesus Christ as your Savior! Believe that He took your sins upon Himself when He died on the cross, and be saved. May God's blessing rest on us all, and may we meet in glory. That is the prayer of my heart!